mastering user surveys

A Comprehensive Guide for UX Designers and Researchers

william webb

contents

1 / introduction to surveys in ux research

the significance of user surveys in ux

AH, the wonderful world of user surveys! You may be wondering, "Why the enthusiasm for something so seemingly mundane?" Well, let's embark on this journey together, and you'll soon understand why.

UX, or User Experience, is all about understanding the user. It's about delving into their thoughts, understanding their behaviors, and empathizing with their needs. But here's the thing: we're not mind readers. This is where user surveys come into play. They act as our window into the minds and hearts of our users, and when done correctly, they can be incredibly revealing.

• • •

Imagine you've designed what you believe to be the perfect user interface. It's sleek, intuitive, and to you, an absolute masterpiece. However, once you release it into the wild, you find that users are getting stuck at a particular step or they're misunderstanding a certain feature. This disconnection between what you believe is perfect and what the user experiences can be bridged using user surveys.

Now, why are user surveys so crucial?

1. Direct Feedback from the Source:

Without user surveys, we're essentially playing a guessing game. Sure, we have design principles and best practices to guide us, but at the end of the day, the user is the true judge. Surveys allow us to hear directly from them. We get their raw, unfiltered thoughts, and that's golden.

2. Cost-Effective Insights:

Imagine having to make changes post-launch because users find a feature challenging. Making such changes can be expensive, both in terms of time and resources. On the other hand, a well-structured survey during the design or testing phase can identify these pain points early on. The earlier we get this feedback, the cheaper and easier it is to make necessary adjustments.

3. Granularity and Depth:

User surveys can be as broad or as specific as you'd like them to be. Need to know if your overall design is appealing? Or perhaps you want to drill down into how users feel about the color scheme of a particular button? Surveys can cater to both these needs and everything in between. The ability to capture both macro and micro insights makes surveys a versatile tool in our UX toolkit.

4. Quantitative and Qualitative Data Mix:

Here's where the beauty of surveys truly shines. Not only can you gather quantifiable data like ratings, rankings, and stats, but you also get qualitative insights. Reading a comment where a user passionately explains why they love (or despise) a feature can offer deeper insights than numbers alone.

• • •

5. Identifying Patterns and Trends:

When you collect data from a large group of users, patterns start to emerge. Maybe a majority find a specific feature unnecessary, or perhaps there's an overwhelming demand for a new function. Recognizing these patterns allows us to focus our design efforts where they matter most.

As we dive deeper into the importance of surveys, it's also crucial to touch upon the concept of "complect conversations." What's that, you ask? Well, "complect" is a term that, in its essence, means to interweave or entwine. In the context of our discussion, it means creating layered, multidimensional conversations with users through surveys. Instead of just skimming the surface, we're diving deep, seeking connections between different pieces of feedback, and understanding the intricate web of user needs and desires.

Now, you might be wondering how to achieve this depth. It starts by crafting questions that prompt users to think and reflect, not just react. Instead of merely asking if they like a feature, ask them to explain why. Encourage them to share stories of how they use a particular function in their daily lives. The richer the conversation, the more valuable the insights.

User surveys, when thoughtfully crafted, can transform our approach to design. They shift our perspective from designing based on assumptions to designing based on genuine user needs. They give voice to the user, ensuring that their opinions, desires, and frustrations are front and center.

But remember, as powerful as user surveys are, they're only one piece of the puzzle. They should be used in conjunction with other UX research methods like usability testing, interviews, and observations. Surveys give us the 'what' and the 'why,' but the holistic picture comes from blending various research methodologies.

when to use surveys in the ux research process

Peering into the diverse toolbox of a UX researcher, one might find an array of tools, each shimmering with its unique purpose and potential. Amid these, the humble user survey stands out - not for its glitz, but for its profound ability to draw connections, insights, and narratives. The previous chapter highlighted the immense power of user surveys. But like any superhero, timing is essential for their efficacy. Knowing when to unleash the might of user surveys is as critical as understanding their potential.

It's the difference between catching a butterfly in your hands or watching it flutter away. Just as you wouldn't pull out a hammer to tighten a screw, you wouldn't deploy a user survey without ensuring it's the right moment in your UX research journey. Let's delve into the key phases when user surveys can be the heroes we need.

1. The Exploration Phase:

Imagine embarking on a journey without a map. Sounds adventurous, right? But also potentially perilous. In the world of UX design, this map is your initial understanding of user needs, preferences, and pain points. Before any design begins, surveys can be utilized to gather broad insights. This is your opportunity to ask open-ended questions and allow respondents to paint a picture of their world for you. You're not looking for validation here; instead, you're seeking to uncover new territories and insights.

• • •

2. Concept Validation:

So, you've got a brilliant idea, a concept that you believe could change the user experience game. But will your users resonate with it? At this juncture, a survey can help gauge initial reactions. While it won't provide the depth of a usability test, it can surely offer a temperature check. If 90% of your users scratch their heads at a concept, it might be worth revisiting.

3. Post-Prototype Feedback:

Once you have a working prototype, it's tempting to jump straight into detailed usability testing. While that's crucial, a user survey can provide initial feedback. By blending both quantitative metrics (like a satisfaction scale) and qualitative insights (like open-ended feedback), you gain a rounded understanding of where your prototype shines and where it might need some polish.

4. After Iterations:

Made changes based on previous feedback? Great! But before you pat yourself on the back, it's time to check back with the users. Surveys, at this stage, can help determine if the changes hit the mark. This cyclical feedback process ensures that user voices remain central to design evolution.

5. Post-Launch Evaluation:

The product is out in the world, being interacted with and hopefully, loved by users. This stage is ripe for surveys that aim to understand overall user satisfaction and identify areas for future improvement. Remember, the UX journey doesn't end with launch; it merely enters a new phase.

Now, about those complect conversations we discussed earlier. When we integrate them into our surveys, they transform from being transactional to relational. No matter which phase you're in, aiming for depth and connection can offer unparalleled insights.

For instance, in the exploration phase, instead of simply asking, "Which features do you use most often?", you might phrase it as, "Can you describe a typical scenario in which you use our platform? What features play a starring role in that experience?" The latter invites a narrative, a story. You're not just collecting data; you're gathering experiences.

Similarly, during concept validation, avoid binary 'yes or no' questions. Opt instead for layered questions that tease out the nuances of user reactions. "How does this concept fit into your daily routine?" or "What emotions does this feature evoke for you?" By allowing users to share more, you're forging a bond with them, making them co-authors in your design story.

These complect conversations are as much an art as they are a science. It's about learning to listen between the lines, to find patterns not just in numbers, but in narratives. As you deploy surveys across different stages, remember that your users are more than just data points; they're storytellers, eager to share their tales. By providing them the platform and inviting depth, you're not only enriching your design process but also valuing the lived experiences of your users.

Every stage of the UX process has its unique challenges and questions. Surveys, when timed right, can be the guiding light, helping researchers navigate the labyrinthine journey of design. And while surveys are undeniably powerful, remember that they are most potent when combined with other research methods. Use them to kickstart conversations, to validate assumptions, and to keep the user narrative alive and evolving.

2 / foundations of effective surveys

the principles of good survey design

JUST AS A CHEF perfects a recipe by blending ingredients in the right proportions, a survey designer must fuse various elements harmoniously. While a poorly designed survey is like a bland dish, a well-crafted one can elicit rich flavors of user insights, especially when seasoned with complect conversations. With that delicious analogy, let's embark on the culinary journey of creating delectable surveys.

1. Clarity Above All:

Remember those cryptic riddles in adventure movies? Fun for treasure hunts, but not for surveys. Questions should be straightforward and devoid of jargon. If a respondent scratches their head, wondering, "What do they mean by this?", you might be losing out on valuable feedback. Let's make it simple and relatable.

2. Be Concise, Be Precise:

Imagine a survey that rambles on like a never-ending tale. By question 50, even the most patient respondent might lose steam. Aim for brevity. Focus on what you truly need to know and craft questions that get straight to the point.

3. Avoid the Double Barrel:

A classic pitfall! Questions like, "Do you find our app intuitive and engaging?" are problematic. What if someone finds it intuitive but not engaging? Split such questions to capture clearer insights.

4. The Magic of Scaling:

Rating scales offer a quantifiable perspective, but they can be tricky. Is 1 good or bad? Always define your scales. And remember, odd-numbered scales (like 1-5) offer a neutral middle ground, while even-numbered ones force a choice. Choose wisely based on what you're aiming to extract.

5. Open-ended Wonders:

Ah, the gateways to complect conversations! Open-ended questions are where respondents can weave their tales. However, use them judiciously. Sprinkle them in areas where you genuinely seek depth, like, "Describe a challenge you often face with our interface." And when they answer, probe further. Dive into the 'whys' and 'hows' of their experiences.

6. Be Mindful of Bias:

Surveys should be neutral canvases, allowing users to paint their truths. Avoid leading questions like, "Don't you love our new feature?" Instead, opt for unbiased phrasing, such as, "How do you feel about our new feature?"

7. Logical Flow is Key:

Imagine being asked about dessert preferences and suddenly, the next question is about appetizers. Disorienting, right? Surveys should flow like well-curated playlists, with one question leading naturally to the next.

8. Make Room for Everyone:

Diversity is the spice of life. Ensure your surveys are inclusive, catering to a wide range of users. Avoid binary options when asking about gender, and always provide an 'Other' or 'Prefer not to say' choice when needed.

9. Testing, 1, 2, 3:

Before launching your survey into the world, test it on a smaller group. This pilot run can help identify confusing questions, technical glitches, or areas that need more depth.

10. Feedback Loop:

While we're keen on gathering feedback, it's also vital to share back. Consider sending respondents a summary of insights or actions based on the survey. It makes them feel valued and completes the conversation loop.

• • •

We've often spoken about complect conversations in our journey, and it's worth reiterating their importance in survey design. A survey isn't merely a transaction; it's an interaction. When respondents share their experiences, feelings, and perspectives, they're inviting you into their world. And what better way to honor this invitation than by engaging deeply?

When you come across a particularly insightful open-ended response, don't let the conversation end there. Reach out, delve deeper. Maybe it's a follow-up question, a thank you note, or an invitation for a more in-depth interview. By doing so, you're telling the respondent, "Hey, I'm listening. Your voice matters."

Think of surveys as bridges. On one side, you have the product or service, brimming with potential and intent. On the other, you have users, teeming with experiences, needs, and stories. A well-designed survey serves as a sturdy bridge, facilitating a dialogue between these two worlds.

avoiding bias: keeping your surveys neutral

Dipping into the world of survey crafting, it's tempting to wish for responses that sing praises or confirm our cherished beliefs. Yet, the true essence of a survey is to be a mirror, reflecting genuine user experiences, feelings, and insights. It shouldn't be a carnival mirror, warping and skewing perceptions. This brings us to the concept of bias in surveys, a sneaky element that can slip in, often unnoticed. Let's navigate this intricate topic, understanding how to keep our surveys as neutral as Switzerland.

1. Recognizing Our Own Biases:

Here's an intriguing thought. We all carry around a backpack of biases, shaped by our experiences, backgrounds, and beliefs. The first step in avoiding bias in surveys is to acknowledge and be aware of our own inherent biases. It's a tad introspective, but it lays the foundation for neutrality.

2. The Craft of Questioning:

How a question is framed can drastically impact the response. Leading questions, like "You found our new feature helpful, didn't you?" already push respondents towards a positive affirmation. Instead, a neutral "How did you find our new feature?" keeps the door open for any genuine feedback.

3. Scale Balance:

When using scales, it's essential to provide a balanced set of options. If you're offering five positive and two negative choices, you're inadvertently nudging respondents towards positivity. An even distribution ensures you're not tilting the scales (pun intended).

4. Ditch the Assumptions:

Questions that begin with assumptions can be limiting. Asking "Why did you love our latest update?" assumes the respondent loved it. It's like asking someone why they adore pineapple pizza without first confirming if they do! A more neutral approach would be, "How did you feel about our latest update?"

5. The Power of Order:

Did you know that the sequence of questions can introduce bias? Often, respondents might be influenced by earlier questions. Randomizing the order for different participants or ensuring a logical flow without leading questions can help mitigate this.

6. Keep Options Open:

When offering multiple choices, it's pivotal to include options like "Other" or "Not Applicable." It ensures respondents aren't shoehorned into selecting choices that don't truly reflect their feelings.

7. Avoiding Double Negatives:

Questions framed with double negatives can confuse respondents. "Don't you dislike our old design?" can throw users into a loop. Simplicity is key. "How did you feel about our old design?" is straightforward and bias-free.

8. Embracing Complect Conversations:

Here's where our favorite concept, complect conversations, comes into play. When a respondent shares feedback, especially through open-ended questions, delve deeper without leading them. For instance, if someone expresses a challenge with your interface, a follow-up like "Can you share more about that experience?" is neutral, inviting depth without swaying their narrative.

Bias, as you might have realized by now, can be a subtle intruder. Yet, with conscious effort, awareness, and meticulous crafting, we can keep our surveys neutral, ensuring they're true reflections of user sentiment.

Let's envision for a moment. Imagine a grand tapestry of user feedback, each thread representing a genuine emotion, a raw experience, or a heartfelt suggestion. Biases are like stains on this tapestry, distracting from its authentic beauty. Our role, as survey crafters, is to ensure that this tapestry remains unsullied, presenting a true mosaic of user voices.

As we wind down this exploration of neutrality and bias in surveys, let's carry forward a promise. A commitment to honor the sanctity of feedback, to respect the individuality of each respondent, and to craft surveys that are as unbiased as possible. Because at the end of the day, a survey's worth is measured not by the affirmations it garners, but by the truths it unveils.

balancing quantitative and qualitative data

Imagine walking into a grand art gallery. On one side, there are precise, geometric artworks – think sharp lines, structured patterns, and clear metrics. On the opposite wall, you're captivated by abstract paintings – swirls of emotions, narratives, and stories waiting to be interpreted. In the survey realm, the world of data collection is pretty much like this gallery. Quantitative data offers the structured clarity, while qualitative data brings in the colors of human experience. Navigating this balance is both an art and a science. Ready to explore?

1. The Pillars of Data: Understanding Quantitative and Qualitative:

First, a brief primer. Quantitative data revolves around numbers. Think of scales, ratings, or any data point that can be measured and crunched into statistics. Qualitative data, on the other hand, is the realm of open-ended responses, anecdotes, and the rich tapestry of human emotions.

• • •

2. Why Both Matter:

One might wonder, "Isn't it enough if I get heaps of numeric data?" While numbers offer clear benchmarks, without the context or stories behind them, they can feel hollow. Similarly, relying solely on qualitative insights without any metrics might leave you adrift in a sea of opinions without a clear direction.

3. The Dance of Depth and Breadth:

Quantitative data provides breadth. You can swiftly see patterns and trends from a large number of respondents. Qualitative data, on the other hand, offers depth. It's like diving into a novel, getting to know characters intimately. In UX, you need both the bird's-eye view and the close-ups.

4. Crafting Questions for Both Worlds:

Quantitative questions are your scales and multiple-choice ones. "On a scale of 1-5, how easy was the checkout process?" However, following this with a qualitative question like, "What did you like or dislike about the checkout process?" ensures you're not just collecting numbers but also the stories behind them.

. . .

5. Analyzing and Interpreting:

This is where the magic happens. Let's say 80% of respondents gave a 4 or 5 to your checkout process. That's a good number. But then, diving into the qualitative responses, you find mentions of a particular step that was confusing. Now, you have a direction for improvement, all thanks to the balance of data.

6. The Role of Complect Conversations:

Remember our theme of complect conversations? This becomes crucial, especially in the qualitative domain. When a respondent shares an anecdote or experience, it opens the door for a deeper dive. Maybe you could reach out for a detailed interview, or perhaps design a follow-up survey based on intriguing qualitative insights.

7. Visualization and Storytelling:

Data, when visualized, becomes more compelling. Pie charts, bar graphs, or heat maps can help stakeholders quickly grasp quantitative insights. But what about qualitative? That's where the art of storytelling comes into play. Crafting personas, weaving narratives, or even creating journey maps can make those abstract insights tangible.

8. The Evolutionary Dance:

Here's something fascinating. Often, qualitative insights from one survey can shape the quantitative questions for the next. For instance, if multiple users pointed out an issue with a particular feature, your next survey could have specific quantitative metrics around that feature.

9. Bringing Stakeholders on Board:

Sometimes, stakeholders might have a preference. "Show me the numbers!" or "Tell me the stories!" As professionals, it becomes our role to emphasize the symbiotic relationship between quantitative and qualitative data. It's about painting the complete picture.

10. Continual Learning:

The world of UX is dynamic. As you iterate and evolve your products or services, the balance of quantitative and qualitative might shift. Being adaptive and understanding when to lean into one more than the other is part of the learning curve.

• • •

Dwelling on the art gallery analogy from earlier, the beauty truly lies in appreciating both the structured geometric patterns and the wild, unrestrained abstracts. They coexist, each enhancing the other's charm.

In our journey through the vast landscape of UX, data is our compass. While quantitative data might show the North Star, guiding the direction, it's the qualitative data that describes the terrain, the weather, and the experiences of past travelers. It's this intertwined dance of logic and emotion, numbers and narratives, that paints a holistic picture.

As we close this chapter, let's take with us the commitment to value both data types. Here's to the stories and statistics, the facts and feelings, and the beautiful balance between them. And remember, as you navigate the realm of UX with this balanced compass, you're well-equipped to craft experiences that truly resonate with the heart and mind. Onward to more insightful journeys!

3 / crafting the perfect questions

question formulation: dos and don'ts

PICTURE THIS: You're setting off on an expedition to unearth the elusive treasure of genuine user insights. Your map? The questions you formulate. Just like any treasure map, the clarity, accuracy, and structure of your questions will determine whether you stumble upon priceless gems or end up on a wild goose chase.

Alright, fellow explorer, let's dive into the intricate world of question formulation. Strap in; it's going to be a revealing journey.

1. DO Start with Clear Objectives:

Before you even pen down that first question, be clear about what you seek to discover. Having a focused objective acts as a guiding star, ensuring your questions remain relevant and purposeful.

2. DON'T Use Jargon or Technical Terms:

Unless you're surveying a group of experts in a specific domain, it's best to keep your language simple. Imagine asking a casual user about "responsive breakpoints" when you simply could ask if the website looks good on both their phone and computer. See the difference?

3. DO Keep Questions Short and Direct:

Lengthy questions can be exhausting. "What are your thoughts about the recent modification we did on our mobile app's user interface in terms of visual appeal and functionality?" Phew! Instead, try: "How do you feel about the recent changes to our app's look and function?"

4. DON'T Ask Double-barreled Questions:

Avoid cramming two questions into one. "Do you like our website's design and navigation?" breaks down into two queries about design and navigation. Respondents might like one aspect and not the other. Split them for clarity!

5. DO Offer a Range of Responses:

For multiple-choice or scaled questions, provide a balanced range of options. It ensures respondents find an option that truly reflects their sentiment.

6. DON'T Lead the Respondent:

Leading questions subtly prompt a specific response. "Don't you think our new feature is ground-breaking?" is loaded with bias. Instead, "How would you describe our new feature?" keeps it neutral.

7. DO Embrace Open-ended Questions for Depth:

Especially when you're after those rich, complect conversations. "Can you share an experience where our product made a difference?" can yield deep insights, personal stories, and invaluable feedback.

8. DON'T Forget the Option of 'Not Applicable':

Sometimes, a question might not resonate with a

respondent due to their unique experience. Always provide an out in such cases. This ensures data accuracy, as respondents aren't forced to choose an irrelevant option.

9. DO Pilot Test Your Questions:

Before releasing your survey into the wild, test it among a smaller group. This trial run can highlight any confusing or misinterpreted questions, giving you a chance to refine them.

10. DON'T Neglect the Power of Sequence:

The flow of your questions matters. Start general, then get specific. Also, ensure sensitive or potentially off-putting questions come later, once the respondent is already engaged.

11. DO Factor in Cultural and Regional Differences:

If your audience is global, nuances in language, cultural references, or even the perception of scales (like 1-5) can vary. Tailoring or being aware of these nuances can be crucial.

• • •

12. DON'T Make Assumptions:

It's easy to project our beliefs onto questions. "Why did you enjoy using our product?" assumes they enjoyed it. Instead, "How was your experience using our product?" keeps it open-ended.

Now, let's connect this back to our theme of complect conversations. Think of every question as a thread. While some threads might lie on the surface, others delve deep, weaving intricate patterns and revealing layers. The art lies in knowing when to tug on which thread and how deep to delve. It's this interplay, this dance between the superficial and the profound, that gives a survey its richness.

Embarking on this quest for user insights, equipped with these dos and don'ts, you're more than ready to chart your course. Your questions are your compass, your lantern, and sometimes even the key to unlock deeper mysteries.

The canvas of user experiences and insights is vast, teeming with stories, emotions, feedback, and nuances.

And every well-crafted question is like a brushstroke, adding depth, color, and clarity to this canvas.

choosing the right question type: open-ended vs. closed-ended

Imagine walking into an ice cream parlor. On one side, you have a sundae bar with a smorgasbord of toppings and flavors, allowing you to craft the perfect dessert. On the other, a menu of pre-made ice cream sandwiches, delightful in their simplicity. Each has its merits, right? It's a bit like choosing between open-ended and closed-ended questions for your survey. Both delicious in their own way, but serving different purposes.

Let's unravel this.

Open-ended Questions: The Sundae Bar

What They Are:

These are the questions without predefined answers. They're free-form, letting respondents pour out their thoughts, feelings, and perspectives, much like choosing every element of that sundae.

The Scoop on Their Strengths:

1. Depth of Insight: Like scooping out the rich gelato at the bottom of the tub, open-ended questions dive deep. They unearth nuanced feedback, stories, and sometimes unexpected revelations.

2. No Leading: Since you're not providing options, respondents aren't swayed or limited by your predefined answers. They have the freedom to express, sprinkle some nuts here, maybe some cherries there; it's all up to them.

3. Ideal for Exploratory Research: If you're at a stage where you're identifying problems or seeking innovation, these questions can be your best pal. Think of them as the first step in your ideation process.

And the Sticky Spots:

• • •

1. Analysis can be Time-Consuming: With a diverse range of answers, sifting through the responses is like trying to find that one candy piece you dropped in your sundae—it requires time and patience.

2. Overwhelming for Some Respondents: Not everyone wants to craft a sundae from scratch. Some might feel the task is too daunting or time-consuming, leading to skipped questions or superficial answers.

Closed-ended Questions: The Ice Cream Sandwich Menu

What They Are:

Questions with set response options. Respondents choose from the given list, much like picking a pre-made ice cream sandwich.

The Sweet Spots of Their Strengths:

1. Efficient and Easy: For both you and the respondent. It's a quick choice, a bite, and they're done. On your

end, analyzing data is as swift as counting the number of sandwiches sold.

2. Quantifiable: Need statistics? Percentages? Graphs? Closed-ended questions are your go-to. They produce quantifiable data that can be easily compared and contrasted.

3. Reduced Ambiguity: With predefined answers, you're less likely to get responses that leave you scratching your head, wondering what they mean.

The Melty Bits to Consider:

1. Limited Depth: It's hard to get the full story when respondents are picking from a list. Sometimes, it's like getting just a taste when you're craving the whole sandwich.

2. Potential for Bias: Since you're setting the options, there's a chance of inadvertently swaying respondents towards a particular choice.

. . .

3. Missing Out: There might be an answer or perspective you haven't considered, and since it's not on your list, you'll never know.

Weaving Them Together for Complect Conversations

Remember that ice cream parlor? It would be a tad boring if it only offered one of the two, right? Similarly, a mix of open and closed-ended questions can often serve you best, especially when aiming for those complect conversations that add layers of understanding.

Start with closed-ended questions to set the stage. These can help respondents ease into the survey and give you some initial quantitative data. Then, as they're warmed up, throw in the open-ended ones. These will encourage respondents to share stories, provide explanations, or express opinions. By blending the two, you're crafting a richer, more insightful narrative of user experiences.

. . .

In essence, it's all about what you aim to discover. If you're looking for precise data, trends, or comparisons, those pre-made ice cream sandwiches (closed-ended questions) might be the way to go. But if you're after the stories, emotions, and unexpected nuggets of wisdom, then dive into that sundae bar (open-ended questions) with gusto.

Surveys are as much art as they are science. And like any good artist, it's essential to know your tools, understand your audience, and craft with intention. Whether you're scooping out gelato, sprinkling toppings, or selecting the perfect ice cream sandwich, remember that the goal is always the same: to understand, engage, and serve your audience better.

phrasing questions for clarity and precision

Remember the time when someone explained something so vaguely that you felt like you were trying to piece together a puzzle in the dark? Or that friend who rambled on, and you just nodded along, not quite catching the gist? Unclear communication is everywhere. But in surveys, ambiguity isn't just inconvenient—it's detrimental. When crafting questions, clarity and precision aren't just ideals; they're requirements.

Dive with me into the world of survey question formulation, where every word can make the difference between a respondent's "Aha!" and "Huh?".

1. Clear as Crystal: The Virtue of Simplicity

It's tempting to show off our extensive vocabulary or be overly formal. But when it comes to surveys, simpler is often better.

Tip: Avoid jargon or technical terms unless you're absolutely certain your respondents are familiar with them. If you're surveying expert users or professionals in a field, certain terms might be okay. Otherwise, stick to plain language.

For example, instead of asking, "Do you utilize mobile banking interfaces regularly?", simplify it to, "Do you use mobile banking often?".

• • •

2. One at a Time, Please: The Single-barreled Approach

Imagine being asked, "Are you happy with your job and commute?" How would you answer if you loved your job but loathed the commute? This is a double-barreled question, and it's a no-go in survey land.

Tip: Focus on one idea per question. If you find yourself using 'and' to combine concepts, it's time to split that question.

3. The Precision of Specificity

While it's essential to be concise, don't sacrifice necessary details. Being specific can guide respondents in giving you the information you're genuinely after.

For instance, "Do you exercise?" is open-ended. "How often do you exercise in a week?" provides a framework for the response you're expecting.

• • •

4. Offer Reference Points

Sometimes, clarity requires a frame of reference, especially with subjective concepts.

Instead of "Do you consider your city to be polluted?", try "Compared to five years ago, do you think the pollution in your city has increased, decreased, or remained the same?"

5. Neutral is the Name of the Game

Phrasing can unintentionally sway respondents. "Don't you think our product is fantastic?" might massage our ego, but it also leads respondents. A neutral "How would you rate our product?" is more genuine.

Tip: Always review questions for potential bias or leading phrasing. If in doubt, get a second opinion.

• • •

6. Get to Know the Negative

Negative phrasing can confuse. A question like, "Don't you dislike when the app crashes?" is a maze of its own. It's unclear whether agreeing means they dislike crashes or if they're okay with them.

Tip: As a rule, avoid negatives. But if you must use them, ensure the meaning remains crystal clear.

7. Making the Implicit, Explicit

Sometimes what's obvious to you might not be for the respondent. If you're looking for a specific type of answer, guide the respondent.

Instead of "How often do you read?", specify with "How many books do you read in a month?"

8. Assume Less, Ask More

. . .

Assumptions can lead to confusion. Instead of asking "How do you like your coffee?", which assumes the respondent drinks coffee, a more inclusive question is "Do you drink coffee? If yes, how do you like it?"

By breaking assumptions, you not only gain clarity but also make the respondent feel acknowledged.

By now, you might be thinking, crafting survey questions sounds a lot like refining a skill. And you'd be spot on. Like a potter perfecting a vase or a chef finetuning a recipe, the nuances matter. Every word, the order, the phrasing—it all culminates in the masterpiece that is a clear, precise survey question.

But don't let that daunt you. With every survey you craft, you'll become more attuned to potential pitfalls and nuances. Each iteration will be clearer and more precise than the last.

Remember, the goal isn't just to ask but to understand. It's a conversation between you and the respondent, albeit in a slightly different format. And like any good conversation, it requires clarity, understanding, and a touch of finesse.

avoiding leading questions and other pitfalls

Picture this: you're at a dinner party, and someone poses a question like, "Isn't it obvious that chocolate ice cream is the best flavor?" The room buzzes with agreement, a few chocolate enthusiasts cheer, but you, a die-hard vanilla fan, feel a tad cornered. That's a leading question in action—a seemingly innocent inquiry that subtly nudges you towards a particular response.

In everyday conversation, such questions can be benign or even humorous. However, in the realm of UX research and surveys, they're unwelcome guests. Not only do leading questions skew results, but they also rob us of genuine insights. Let's unravel this intriguing issue, shall we?

1. Recognizing Leading Questions

• • •

The first step to avoiding a pitfall is knowing what it looks like. Leading questions often:

- Assume a particular answer: "You found our app's interface user-friendly, didn't you?"
- Use emotive language: "How frustrated did you feel with the slow-loading website?"
- Offer limited choices: "Did our product improve your efficiency a lot or just a bit?"

Did you see the subtle push in each example? It's like handing someone an ice cream cone but only offering chocolate or strawberry—sorry, vanilla fans!

2. Crafting Neutral Alternatives

To extract authentic feedback, frame your questions neutrally. Taking the previous examples:

- Instead of assuming: "How would you describe our app's interface?"
- Remove the emotive push: "How would you describe your experience with the website's loading speed?"

- Expand choices: "How has our product impacted your efficiency?"

See the difference? By providing a neutral platform, you invite a range of genuine responses.

3. The Double-Barreled Trouble

Another pitfall is the double-barreled question, which we brushed upon in a previous chapter. It's like asking two questions but allowing for one answer, causing confusion. "Did you find our website informative and easy to navigate?" Hold up! What if it was informative but hard to navigate?

Tip: When reviewing your questions, watch for the sneaky 'and' that often signals you're asking about two concepts. Split such questions to ensure clarity.

4. The Assumption Abyss

• • •

"During your weekly shopping at our store..." Wait a minute! What if they shop monthly? Assuming frequency, behaviors, or preferences can alienate respondents or force them into inaccurate responses.

Always structure questions that give room for varied experiences: "How often do you shop at our store?"

5. Loaded Questions: The Hidden Agenda

This one's tricky. Loaded questions carry an implicit assumption, often linked with societal norms or expectations. "Have you stopped overeating?" assumes the person was overeating in the first place.

Tip: Always take a step back and review your questions for any inherent biases or assumptions. When in doubt, rephrase.

6. Beware of the Absolute

• • •

Questions that employ absolutes like "always" or "never" can corner respondents. "Do you always understand our app's instructions?" Such absolutes can lead to inaccurate feedback since life (and user experience) rarely deals in absolutes.

It's more productive to ask, "How often do you find our app's instructions clear?"

7. Overcome the Yes/No Overreliance

Yes/No questions have their place, but leaning on them too much can rob you of richer insights. Rather than "Did you like our tutorial?", which gives a binary answer, "What did you think of our tutorial?" can yield deeper feedback.

Now, let's pause for a second. If this feels like a lot, take a deep breath. No one crafts the perfect survey overnight. But every misstep, every leading question you spot in hindsight, makes you better for the next round. And trust me, that learning curve? It's worth every twist and turn.

. . .

As we sail towards the end of this chapter, imagine the potential of the surveys you'll craft. Think of the clarity, the genuine insights, and the deeper understanding you'll unearth—all because you took the time to learn about these pitfalls.

Surveys are a dialogue—a chance to listen, learn, and connect with users. And with every question you craft, you're not just gathering data; you're building bridges. And while you might have an occasional leading question sneak in or an assumption you overlook, remember that growth is a journey. It's the commitment to authenticity, to truly hearing your respondents, that will set your surveys apart.

iterative testing and refining of questions

Let's begin with a thought experiment. Imagine crafting the perfect clay pot. You have the finest clay, a spinning wheel, and your artist's intent. You mold the clay, give it a shape, and after a while, you get a version of what you imagined. But does the pot sit perfectly? Are there any bumps or imperfections? Does it wobble when placed on a flat surface?

This scenario isn't too different from crafting survey questions. Your initial draft might capture the essence of what you want, but there's a high likelihood it could benefit from a little refinement. And just like the art of pottery, creating the perfect survey question requires iteration—testing and refining.

1. The Value of Iterative Testing

Picture your survey as the clay pot. It's the vessel carrying your inquiry, and its form is essential for the substance it will hold—the responses. Now, if a pot has a slight lean or a tiny bump, it might still function. But perfection, in pottery and surveys, is a blend of form and function. It's all about ensuring that every curve, every nuance, works seamlessly.

Similarly, when a survey question is slightly off-mark or ambiguous, it may still fetch an answer. However, to extract precise, actionable insights, the question needs to be sculpted just right.

2. The Test Run: The Pilot Survey

Before sending out your survey to hundreds or thousands of potential respondents, consider a smaller pilot run. This initial feedback can highlight ambiguities, biases, or other problem areas in your questions.

Feedback from a pilot survey provides two critical insights:

- Clarity checks: Do respondents understand your questions as intended?
- Relevance checks: Are the questions resonating with the respondents' experiences?

Remember, this isn't about merely collecting data. It's about ensuring that when you do cast a wider net, every question is fine-tuned to perfection.

3. Incorporate Feedback

. . .

Here's where the art of iteration truly shines. Analyze feedback from your pilot survey not as criticism but as guidance. Look for patterns:

- Are multiple respondents getting tripped up on the same question?
- Are any questions consistently skipped or left unanswered?

Such patterns can indicate where a question might need rewording or, perhaps, removal.

4. The Power of A/B Testing

Another exciting technique to refine your questions is A/B testing. Consider crafting two versions of a potentially problematic question and testing them on different subsets of your pilot group. Analyze which version fetches more accurate or clearer responses. A/B testing can be an enlightening exercise in understanding the nuances of phrasing and question structure.

5. Refinement isn't Just Reduction

As you sift through feedback and spot areas of improvement, remember that refining isn't just about trimming or simplifying. Sometimes, a question might need elaboration or a brief explanation. Other times, a single question might be better split into two to garner more specific insights.

6. Iteration Beyond Questions

While our focus here is on iterative testing of questions, don't forget the broader aspects of your survey. For instance:

- Is the survey's flow intuitive?
- Are there technical glitches or interface issues that might disrupt the respondent's experience?
- Is the length of the survey appropriate, or does it

risk respondent fatigue?

Considering these broader elements ensures that when respondents engage with your survey, they have a seamless experience.

Let's come full circle, back to our pottery analogy. Crafting the perfect clay pot, much like crafting the ideal survey, is a dance of patience and persistence. It's about understanding that the first version, while filled with potential, can always be improved upon. And each iteration, each small refinement, takes you one step closer to perfection.

As UX professionals, our goal is always to understand our users better. And surveys are a potent tool in this endeavor. However, the power of a survey doesn't just lie in the questions posed, but in the meticulous crafting and refining of those questions. It's in the recognition that every survey sent out is a conversation started—a dialogue with the user. And for a conversation to be truly fruitful, we must ensure that every question we pose is clear, precise, and designed to elicit genuine insights.

4 / survey flow and structure

the importance of logical flow

EVER BEEN part of a chat where topics switch at lightning speed, leaving you a tad disoriented? Maybe you started talking about movies and then suddenly, without any smooth transition, you found yourselves debating the merits of various cuisines. It can be jarring, right? Similarly, imagine entering an intricate labyrinth without a map or walking a trail without markers. Such experiences can be frustrating and confusing.

That's the sentiment a survey participant can feel when the questions they encounter lack a logical flow. Crafting a survey isn't merely about jotting down a list of queries you'd like answered. It's about guiding your respondent through a structured journey—a dance of dialogue where each step follows the previous in harmony.

1. Logical Flow: Setting The Stage For Conversations

Think of a survey as a storytelling session. You're the narrator, and your respondent is the keen listener. Now, you wouldn't introduce the climax of your story before setting the scene, would you? Likewise, a survey should unravel in layers, gently guiding the respondent from one topic to another.

By ensuring a logical progression, you respect the respondent's cognitive load, making the process more intuitive and less mentally taxing. This, in turn, can lead to more thoughtful and accurate responses.

2. Creating a Smooth Onboarding

Start your survey with easy-to-answer questions that set the context and make the respondent feel comfortable. Much like a warm-up before a workout, this eases them into the process, prepping them for more complex or thought-provoking questions that might follow.

3. Grouping Related Questions

Categorize your questions based on themes or topics and ensure that similar ones stay together. This helps in two ways:

- It allows respondents to focus on one aspect at a time, reducing cognitive jumps.

- It ensures consistency in responses as they are in the same frame of mind when answering related questions.

4. The Pyramid Structure

Visualize your survey as a pyramid. Start broad at the base and gradually narrow down. Begin with general questions and then delve into specifics as you move along. This helps in setting a rhythm and makes the respondent's journey predictable, creating a sense of ease and comfort.

5. Transitions Matter

Imagine reading a book where chapters don't flow into one another. It'd be disorienting, right? The same principle applies to surveys. Introduce transitional statements or brief explanations when shifting from one topic to another. This not only helps in signposting but also preps the respondent for what's to come.

6. Limiting Fatigue: Logical Flow's Unsung Merit

An unpredictable survey can be tiring. When the brain constantly tries to grasp the context or understand the reason behind a question, fatigue can set in. A logical flow, by offering a clear pathway, can significantly reduce this mental strain, ensuring that respondents stay engaged till the very end.

7. Feedback: The Flow's Best Friend

Always be open to feedback. Consider pilot testing your survey with a small group before finalizing it.

Their experience can offer invaluable insights into how seamless the flow feels, allowing you to tweak and refine as needed.

Ah, the end of our conversation on logical flow, or should I say, a gentle amble through the intricacies of crafting seamless surveys? Remember, every interaction, be it a face-to-face chat or a digital survey, thrives on rhythm. It's the harmony, the dance of dialogue, that turns an ordinary exchange into a memorable experience.

Surveys, in the vast world of UX, are our bridge to understanding—our tether to the myriad souls who interact with our creations. By ensuring a logical flow, we honor their time, respect their cognitive space, and pave the way for genuine, insightful responses.

grouping related questions

Have you ever tried assembling a puzzle? There's a certain joy in finding pieces that fit together perfectly, gradually creating a cohesive image from scattered elements. When constructing a survey, think of each question as a piece of this puzzle. You wouldn't scatter them haphazardly, would you? Instead, you'd meticulously group related questions, letting the story unfold organically, capturing the participant's attention and guiding them through with ease.

The Beauty of Cohesive Groupings

Imagine walking into a library where all genres of books are randomly mixed. How tiring would it be to locate your favorite mystery novel amidst cookbooks and historical biographies? That's what it feels like for a respondent navigating a survey with questions scattered without any logic or sequence.

Grouping related questions serves two main purposes:

1. Creating a Conversational Rhythm: Just as a novel takes you from one chapter to the next, each building upon the last, a well-structured survey crafts a narrative that feels natural.

2. Enhancing Response Quality: When similar questions cluster together, respondents don't have to continually shift their mental frameworks. They can delve deeper into a specific topic, offering richer and more nuanced answers.

The Layers of Logical Grouping

1. Topic-Based Clusters: This is the most common way of grouping. For instance, in a product feedback survey, you might start with questions about the product's usability, then transition into its aesthetics, followed by queries about customer support.

2. Complexity Gradation: Sometimes, it's about the mental gear-shifting. Begin with broader, easier-to-answer questions and slowly delve into more specific

or complex areas. This technique often helps in gradually immersing the respondent into the survey.

3. Behavioral Segmentation: Tailor your survey for different user actions. For example, in an app feedback survey, first group questions for those who've used a particular feature, then those who haven't. This ensures each user's journey remains relevant to their experience.

The Art of Transitioning Between Groups

While clustering similar questions is crucial, how you transition from one group to another is equally vital. Here's where a little narrative finesse comes into play:

1. Signposting: A brief sentence or two can effectively signal a shift from one topic to the next. For instance, after a set of questions about a product's usability, you might introduce the next section with, "Now, let's chat about how our product looks and feels to you."

2. Use Pacing Tools: Visual breaks, like horizontal lines or subtle shading differences, can delineate sections in longer surveys, offering respondents a visual cue that they're transitioning to a different topic.

3. Consistency in Transition: While it's tempting to be creative with transitions, maintaining a uniform style throughout the survey reduces cognitive friction.

Pitfalls to Dodge

- Avoid Over-Segmentation: While grouping is crucial, overdoing it can lead to a fragmented experience. If your survey has too many sections with just one or two questions each, consider consolidating.

- Beware of Grouping Bias: Ensuring related questions stay together is essential, but be mindful. Placing too many similar sentiment questions consecutively might inadvertently push the respondent towards a specific answer.

- Test, Test, Test: The real judge of whether your grouping is effective? A fresh pair of eyes. Piloting your survey with a smaller audience can provide insights into the naturalness of your flow.

Grouping related questions isn't merely a structural necessity—it's an art. An art that transforms a mundane questionnaire into an engaging conversation. It's the difference between a hodgepodge of notes and a symphony. And remember, while the science of survey construction is filled with best practices and guidelines, there's always room for intuition and creativity.

branching and skip logic: advanced survey flow techniques

Picture this: you're taking a scenic drive, and you come to a fork in the road. One path leads to the mountains, another to the beach, and yet another to a dense forest. You pick one, and the journey adjusts itself to the choice you made. What if I told you that surveys could offer a similar branching experience, where the respondent's journey varies based on their responses? Welcome to the dynamic world of branching and skip logic!

Diving into Branching

Branching is the survey equivalent of those 'Choose Your Own Adventure' books. Instead of a linear, one-size-fits-all path, respondents follow a route sculpted by their own answers. It ensures they only see questions relevant to them, enhancing the survey's precision and the user's experience.

For instance, if a respondent indicates they've never used a particular product feature, it makes little sense to barrage them with detailed questions about it. Instead, with branching, they'll seamlessly move to questions about aspects they are familiar with.

The Magic of Skip Logic

While branching lets you usher respondents down different paths, skip logic is a tad more subtle. Think of it as a gracious host, subtly guiding a guest past a room they needn't enter. Skip logic allows you to jump over irrelevant questions based on previous answers.

Imagine you're surveying about dietary habits. If a respondent identifies as vegetarian, skip logic ensures they don't get questions about their favorite meats but moves them directly to, perhaps, questions about their favorite vegetables or plant-based proteins.

Crafting the Perfect Flow: Tips and Tricks

1. Plan Meticulously: Before setting up branching or skip logic, map out the journey on paper or digital tools. Visualizing the paths ensures a seamless experience for the respondent.

2. Be Transparent: It's courteous to let respondents know the survey might adjust based on their answers. A simple, "Based on your responses, the next set of questions might vary," works wonders.

3. Keep Branches Balanced: If one path has ten questions and another just one, it might create an uneven experience. Aim for a semblance of balance to ensure every respondent spends a somewhat equal time on the survey.

When to Use (and When to Avoid) These Techniques

Branching and skip logic are potent tools, but they aren't universally suitable.

- Use When Seeking Detailed Insights: If your survey aims to dive deep into specific areas based on user behavior or preferences, branching is invaluable. For product feedback, understanding distinct user experiences, or deep-diving into subsets of a larger audience, these techniques shine.

- Avoid in Broad Overviews: If your survey is about gathering a general consensus or broad feedback, adding too many branches can overcomplicate the process and dilute the data.

The Potential Pitfalls

Like any tool, if used without understanding or foresight, branching and skip logic can lead to complications.

- The Risk of Over-Complication: Too many branches or excessive skipping can make the back-end of data analysis a nightmare. It can also confuse respondents if not implemented seamlessly.

- Missing Broader Insights: By narrowing down the respondent's journey too much, you might miss out on broader insights or unexpected feedback that a more open-ended approach could capture.

- Technical Glitches: Ensure your survey platform can handle the complexity. There's nothing worse than a respondent being stuck due to a technical hiccup.

Alright, let's step back for a moment. Branching and skip logic are a bit like those advanced settings on a camera. In the right hands, under the right conditions, they can produce a masterpiece. Used without thought, they might just lead to a blurry mess. The key? Balance. Understanding when to deploy these tools, and when to rely on simpler structures.

As you craft your surveys, consider the respondent's journey. How can you make it engaging, relevant, yet efficient? Sometimes, this might mean a complex web of branches and skips. At other times, a straight road does the trick. But always remember, the heart of any survey is the conversation between you and the respondent. Every choice you make should enhance that dialogue, make it richer, more genuine, and more insightful.

ending on the right note: the final questions and thank you pages

Ever been to a captivating concert, where the final number leaves you with a haunting melody that lingers in your mind long after the performance ends? That's the kind of lasting impression you want your survey to have on its respondents. The final moments of your survey are just as crucial, if not more so, than the introduction. This isn't just about good manners; it's about ensuring that you leave a positive impression, foster trust, and set the stage for future engagements.

The Power of the Last Question

The questions at the end of a survey, quite like the climax of a novel, can leave an indelible mark. Let's delve into the nuances of framing that perfect last question:

1. Summarize and Reflect: Your final question should offer respondents a chance to reflect on the survey's topic. Maybe it's an open-ended question that lets them share their holistic views, something they might not have been able to communicate in the structured format of previous questions.

2. Personal Connection: Give respondents an opportunity to share how they feel. A simple "How did this survey make you feel?" can provide insights into their emotional response, offering a gauge of their engagement and satisfaction levels.

3. Feedback on the Survey Itself: This is gold! Asking respondents for feedback on the survey's length, structure, or clarity can offer invaluable insights for future refinements.

Thank You Pages: More Than Just a Courtesy

Now, after the curtain falls on the final question, comes the encore – the Thank You page. This is not just a page; it's an opportunity.

1. Show Genuine Gratitude: A sincere thank-you can make respondents feel valued. It acknowledges the time and effort they've given you, reinforcing the idea that their opinion matters.

2. Offer a Recap or Insight: Consider sharing a tidbit of what you aim to achieve with the data collected. "With your help, we aim to improve our

product line in the coming months!" This provides a sense of contribution and involvement.

3. Engage Further: The Thank You page can be a launchpad. Maybe you have another survey coming up, an upcoming product launch, or an informative blog post they might find interesting. Provide links or sign-ups, turning a static thank you into an interactive experience.

4. Feedback Loop: Give them an option to join a mailing list or a feedback loop where they can see the changes or results driven by the survey. This fosters a sense of continuity.

5. Stay Open: Provide a way for respondents to reach out, perhaps through a contact link or a helpline. This extends the dialogue, signaling that their voice is always welcome.

The Dos and Don'ts

- Do personalize the thank you message. If you've collected names, use them. "Thank you, Alex, for your insights!" feels far more personal than a generic thanks.

- Don't overwhelm with too much on the Thank You page. While engagement opportunities are great, you don't want to make it feel cluttered or pushy.

- Do test the links or any interactive elements you embed. A broken link can sour the entire experience.

- Don't miss out on mobile optimization. Many respondents might be accessing your survey on the go.

Ensure your Thank You page is as visually appealing and functional on mobile as it is on desktop.

Remember, ending on the right note isn't just about wrapping up the current conversation; it's about paving the way for future ones. As the saying goes, "People will forget what you said, people will forget what you did, but people will never forget how you made them feel." In the realm of surveys, this rings especially true.

5 / designing surveys for engagement

visual design principles for surveys

HAVE you ever stumbled upon a survey that was so cluttered or jarring that you instantly clicked away? Or perhaps, you've been drawn into a survey purely because of its sleek design and visual appeal? In both cases, the visual design played a pivotal role in your response. Visual design isn't just the cherry on top of your survey sundae—it's an essential ingredient that can either sweeten the experience or leave a bitter aftertaste.

Just like in web design, art, or even fashion, certain principles guide the visual construction of surveys. But before you conjure images of needing a degree in graphic design, let's debunk that notion. With a few fundamental principles and a sprinkling of creativity, anyone can craft a visually compelling survey.

1. Consistency is Key

Uniformity creates familiarity. Whether it's the font, color scheme, or button design, ensure a consistent look throughout your survey. This doesn't mean monotony; it means a cohesive visual theme. For instance:

- Fonts: Stick to a maximum of two fonts—one for headers and one for body text. Ensure they're legible across devices.

- Colors: Choose a primary color for main elements and a secondary color for accents. Using a color wheel can help identify complementary shades.

2. Embrace White Space

Cramming questions together might seem like a way to make your survey concise, but it often overwhelms respondents. White space, or the empty space around your content, isn't wasted space. It gives the content room to "breathe", guiding the respondent's eyes and improving readability.

3. Use Visuals Sparingly but Smartly

Images and videos can enrich your survey, but they should add value, not distract.

- Supporting Visuals: Use images that directly support or clarify your questions. If asking about a product, display its image.

- Avoid Decorative Fluff: Background images or decorative icons that don't serve a purpose can clutter your survey. If it doesn't enhance understanding, reconsider its inclusion.

4. Prioritize Mobile Optimization

With the world increasingly on-the-go, many respondents might access your survey from a mobile device.

- Responsive Design: Ensure your survey's design adjusts to different screen sizes, offering a seamless experience across devices.

- Thumb-friendly Design: Buttons should be large enough for easy tapping, and crucial elements should be within easy thumb reach.

5. Logical Grouping

Group related questions or options together. This can be achieved using boxes, different background colors, or simply spacing. Visual divisions can help respondents quickly grasp the structure and flow, making the survey feel less daunting.

6. Highlight Important Elements

Whether it's a critical question or a call-to-action button, make it stand out. This could be through contrasting colors, bold fonts, or an enclosing shape. But remember, if everything shouts for attention, nothing is heard.

7. Test for Accessibility

Not everyone experiences visuals in the same way. Consider those with color blindness or visual impairments:

- Color Contrast: Ensure text is legible against its background. Tools online can help check contrast ratios.

- Descriptive Texts: If using images, provide alternative text descriptions for those using screen readers.

8. Feedback & Progression Indicators

Let respondents know where they are in the survey and how much is left. Progress bars, percentage counters, or even simple "Question 5 of 10" indicators can make a world of difference. Also, visual feedback, like a color change on button click, can confirm actions, assuring respondents of their inputs.

Imagine the survey as a conversation. You wouldn't want to converse in a noisy, chaotic environment, right? The same goes for surveys. A cluttered, inconsistent design can muddle the conversation, while a clean, engaging design can facilitate a smooth dialogue.

And while we often hear the phrase "don't judge a book by its cover", the reality is, first impressions matter. Especially in the digital realm, where attention spans are fleeting, your survey's visual design is often the first handshake, the introductory smile. Make it inviting, clear, and pleasant.

using interactive elements responsibly

Ah, the digital age! A time when the boundaries of what we can achieve with a simple survey have expanded beyond the checkboxes and radio buttons of yesteryears. Today's surveys can be jazzed up with a variety of interactive elements—from drag-and-drop features to sliders and even multimedia clips. However, with great power (to engage and entertain) comes great responsibility (to not overwhelm or mislead).

When wielded with care, interactive elements can elevate the respondent's experience, making the survey not just a task, but an engaging activity. Yet, without discretion, these elements can just as easily distract, confuse, or alienate. Let's navigate this fine line together.

1. Always Prioritize Clarity

The primary purpose of any survey is to gather reliable data. An interactive element should never come at the expense of clarity. If you're introducing a novel interaction—for instance, a new type of slider or a unique ranking system—provide clear instructions. Make sure the respondent knows exactly how to interact with the element and what their interaction signifies.

2. Enhance, Don't Distract

Imagine you're deep in thought, answering a poignant question about workplace dynamics, and suddenly a flashy animation pops up. Jarring, right? Use animations and transitions sparingly. While they can guide attention or offer a momentary visual respite, they shouldn't disrupt the thought process.

3. Test Load Times

While a short video or an animated graph might seem like a great idea on your super-fast office broadband, consider users who might be on slower connections. An interactive element that causes significant lag can be a source of frustration, leading to survey abandonment. It's crucial to optimize media for web delivery and always provide an alternative for those unable to access the interactive component.

4. Ensure Mobile Compatibility

Many respondents might be accessing your survey on mobile devices. Not all interactive elements that work seamlessly on desktop translate well to mobile. Touchscreens, smaller display sizes, and varied device capabilities demand that you double-check compatibility and usability.

5. Offer Opt-Outs

Regardless of how engaging an interactive element is, always give respondents the option to bypass it if they wish. Whether it's a multimedia segment they'd rather not load or an interaction they find confusing, ensure there's an alternative way to provide their input.

6. Remember Accessibility

Just as with visual design, interactivity must account for all users, including those with disabilities. For instance, a drag-and-drop might be challenging for someone with motor difficulties. Screen readers should be able to interpret and narrate the content of interactive elements. Whenever introducing a novel interaction, think about its accessibility implications.

7. Limit Novelty

It's tempting to use the latest interactive feature you stumbled upon, but here's a mantra to remember: Just because you can, doesn't mean you should. A survey packed with various interactive features can feel gimmicky. Stick to a few consistent types of interactions throughout your survey to maintain a cohesive feel.

8. Feedback is Your Friend

Interactive elements, by nature, involve a two-way street of input and response. If a user moves a slider or selects an interactive image, provide subtle feedback to acknowledge their action. It could be a slight color change, a soft click sound, or a tiny vibration on mobile devices.

We're in a golden age of digital interactivity. The

possibilities are endless, and it's genuinely exciting to think of the ways we can engage respondents. However, the heart of a survey remains its questions and the insights they yield.

As you sprinkle interactive magic onto your surveys, keep the respondent's experience at the forefront of your mind. Interactivity should feel like a natural enhancement, not a hurdle or a spectacle.

Think of your survey as a river, flowing towards the ocean of insights. Interactive elements can be the gentle curves and playful whirlpools that make the journey enjoyable. But if not crafted responsibly, they can also be the rocks and blockages disrupting the flow. Your task, as the survey designer, is to ensure smooth sailing

keeping respondents engaged and preventing dropouts

Picture this: You've spent hours crafting the perfect survey, ensuring every question is poised to extract the golden insights you're after. But halfway through, a respondent's enthusiasm wanes, their attention drifts, and just like that, they're gone. This is the infamous survey dropout, and it's the stuff of nightmares for professionals like us. But fear not! There are proven strategies to keep respondents engaged from start to finish.

1. Start with a Bang

First impressions matter. Kick things off with an engaging question that's easy to answer. It acts like a warm-up, setting the tone for the rest of the survey. If a respondent finds the first question intriguing or relatable, they're more likely to continue with the same momentum.

2. Respect Their Time

You might have a hundred questions, but consider the respondent's perspective. Can they realistically answer all of them in a single sitting without feeling exhausted? Be upfront about how long the survey will take. And if it's on the lengthier side, consider offering a 'save and continue later' option.

3. Mix It Up

Variety is the spice of life and surveys! Alternate between different types of questions—multiple choice, Likert scales, open-ended. This switch in formats can keep respondents on their toes and engaged. Just remember the previous chapter's lesson on "Using interactive elements responsibly".

4. Progress Bars are Magic

There's something deeply satisfying about watching a progress bar fill up. It gives respondents a visual cue of how far they've come and how much further they need to go. This tangible sense of progress can be motivating and reduce the chances of them bowing out early.

5. Be Conversational

Remember, there's a real person on the other end of that survey. Craft your questions as if you're having a face-to-face chat over coffee. Ditch the jargon and keep the language simple and relatable.

6. Limit Mandatory Questions

Sure, there are some questions that you absolutely must have answers to. But if a respondent feels trapped or forced to answer something they're uncomfortable with, they're more likely to exit. Strike a balance. Make the essential questions mandatory, but give them a bit of wiggle room elsewhere.

7. Offer Incentives, But Be Genuine

Who doesn’t love a good incentive? Whether it's a discount, a chance to enter a raffle, or even just the promise of seeing the results of the survey, incentives can be compelling. But here’s the catch: make sure they're genuine. Nothing feels worse than being promised a reward that never materializes.

8. Regularly Test and Refine

Even with all these strategies in play, there's no one-size-fits-all solution. Regularly gather feedback about the survey experience and be ready to tweak based on this input. This iterative approach ensures your survey stays fresh and respondent-friendly.

9. The Power of Pacing

Structure your survey in a way that groups lighter questions together, providing a breather before diving into more in-depth or personal topics. Think of it as a rhythm; a balance between fast-paced sections and slower, reflective ones.

10. End with a Gesture of Appreciation

Once respondents have traveled the length of your survey, show them some love. A thank-you note, perhaps accompanied by a fun fact or a sneak peek into how their input will be used, can leave them with a positive feeling.

Engaging respondents is half art, half science. On the one hand, you're diving deep into the mechanics of survey design and user experience. On the other, you're empathizing with the respondent, understanding their mindset, and offering them a pleasant journey through your questions.

The goal? To transform the mundane act of ticking boxes and typing out answers into an engaging conversation. One where the respondent feels heard, valued, and, most importantly, willing to stay with you till the very end.

6 / the art of screener surveys

the purpose of a screener survey

IMAGINE SETTING up an extravagant dinner party. You've got your favorite dishes prepared, the room adorned with perfect lighting, and a playlist that would make any guest sway. But here's the catch: you don't want just anyone coming in. You want guests who appreciate the specific cuisine you're serving. This is where a good old bouncer comes in handy. They'll ensure only those who truly cherish the taste and ambiance you're offering get a seat at the table.

Now, shift this scenario to the world of research. Your main survey is the dinner party, and a screener survey? Well, that's your trusty bouncer.

The Role of a Screener

A screener survey, as its name suggests, is a preliminary questionnaire used to screen potential participants for your primary research. If your main survey is a deep dive into the ocean, consider the screener as those first few tests of the water with your toes – checking the temperature, ensuring it's right for the dive.

Why Use a Screener Survey?

1. Target Specific Demographics: Suppose you're researching the effects of a new online education platform designed specifically for retirees. Naturally, you wouldn't want responses from college students. A screener can ensure you're hearing from the right age group.

2. Save Time and Resources: Instead of sifting through a plethora of unsuitable respondents later on, you're setting the stage right from the start. You get to invest time in analyzing relevant data, rather than discarding what doesn't fit.

3. Higher Quality Data: By ensuring that respondents meet specific criteria, the data you collect is more likely to be relevant, accurate, and insightful.

Crafting an Effective Screener

Now that you grasp the 'why,' let's jump into the 'how'.

a) Keep it Short: A screener is like an elevator pitch; it's brief and to the point. You want to determine if the respondent is a good fit without taking up too much of their time.

b) Use Simple Language: Avoid jargon or complex phrases. Remember, the goal is to identify if they qualify for the main survey, not to test their vocabulary.

c) Multiple Choice Works Best: They're quick to answer, and easy for you to analyze. Questions like "Which age bracket do you fall into?" or "How often do you use online learning platforms?" can swiftly guide your selection process.

d) Be Discreet: Sometimes, being too direct can influence the respondent's answers. Instead of asking, "Are you a retiree looking to learn online?", you might opt for: "What's your employment status?" followed by, "Are you interested in online courses?"

e) Ensure Privacy: Reassure respondents that their information is confidential. It's about building trust right from the get-go.

Acting on Screener Results

After potential respondents have taken your screener survey, it's decision time.

Qualified Respondents: Send them an invitation to your main survey, perhaps with a note of appreciation for their time and explaining why they're a great fit.

Unqualified Respondents: A gentle note thanking them for their interest and time, while explaining they might not be the perfect fit for this specific study, is courteous. And who knows? They might be the perfect participant for your next project.

To Screen or Not to Screen

Not every survey will require a screener. Sometimes, casting a wide net can provide unexpected and valuable insights. However, when you have a clear, specific target audience in mind, and you're looking to gather deep insights from that group, screeners are your best friend.

targeting the right audience: inclusion and exclusion criteria

Ah, the art of selection! It's not just about whom you invite to the party, but also who might not be a fit for that specific soirée. It's akin to casting for a play. While someone might be a fantastic actor, they might not be suited for every role. Similarly, when it comes to surveys, understanding whom you're speaking to (and whom you're not) can make all the difference in the world. Let's explore the nuances of inclusion and exclusion criteria and how they shape your research.

Why Does Your Audience Matter?

Think of your research as a tailored suit. For it to fit perfectly, you need the right measurements. Your audience is those measurements. The more precise you are in choosing them, the better the fit of your data. A mismatched audience can distort your results, leading you down paths of decision-making that might not be beneficial.

Inclusion Criteria: Rolling Out the Red Carpet

This is your list of must-haves. It defines who needs to be part of your survey for you to gather the insights you seek. These can range from age, profession, geographic location, to even specific behaviors or experiences.

For instance:

- Age: Between 25 and 40
- Uses online banking at least once a week
- Has made an international transaction in the last six months

These criteria ensure your survey is laser-focused on the group you believe will provide the insights you need.

Exclusion Criteria: The Delicate Art of Filtering Out

While it sounds negative, exclusion criteria are just as crucial. This helps you filter out respondents who might skew your data or provide irrelevant information.

Let's continue with our earlier example:

- Anyone below 20 and above 50 years of age
- People who have never used online banking

- Those who only use banking for savings and have never made a transaction

Being clear on your exclusion criteria can streamline your research process and keep your data clean and relevant.

Striking the Balance

At the crossroads of inclusion and exclusion lies balance. While you want to hone in on a specific group, being overly restrictive might narrow down your audience pool too much, making it hard to gather substantial data. Conversely, being too broad might dilute the quality of your insights. Here are a few pointers:

1. Be Clear on Your Research Goals: What do you hope to achieve? The clearer you are on this, the better you can define your audience.

2. Periodic Reviews: As you begin gathering data, it's a good idea to periodically review your criteria. Maybe you need to adjust them a bit based on early insights.

3. Embrace Diversity: While it's essential to have specific criteria, ensure you're not unintentionally excluding diverse voices that might offer fresh perspectives.

Drafting with Precision

When putting together your inclusion and exclusion criteria:

a) Prioritize: While it might be tempting to have a laundry list of criteria, prioritize what's essential.

b) Avoid Overlap: Ensure that your inclusion and exclusion criteria don't contradict each other. For instance, if you're including people aged 25-40, there's no need to exclude those aged 20-30.

c) Stay Open to Feedback: Especially in the early stages, discuss your criteria with colleagues or mentors. Fresh eyes might spot something you missed.

Conclusion: The Perfect Ensemble

Choosing your audience using precise inclusion and exclusion criteria is like assembling a choir. Each voice, each note matters. But to create a harmonious melody, you need to ensure each member complements the other. By being meticulous in this selection, you set the stage (or in our case, the survey) for rich, insightful data that truly sings!

crafting effective screener questions

You've likely experienced that feeling of walking into a room and wondering if you're in the right place. Imagine survey respondents feeling that way. Now, imagine having a polite, concise usher at the door, ensuring only the right people enter and feel at home. That's the magic of screener questions. They ensure that your data is coming from the right sources, making your findings relevant and actionable.

Diving right in, screener questions are the gatekeepers of your survey. Like a bouncer at a swanky club, they determine who gets to participate and who doesn't, based on the criteria you've set. But crafting these questions is both an art and a science.

What Makes Screener Questions Unique?

Unlike other questions in your survey, screeners have a clear-cut job: qualify or disqualify respondents. Their clarity and precision are paramount. Think of them as the first impression of your survey. Messing up here can skew your data in unimaginable ways.

Guidelines for Crafting Your Screeners

1. Keep It Simple and Clear:

Remember, this is the starting point. If respondents get bogged down here, there's a good chance they might not proceed. Avoid jargon or overly technical terms.

2. Be Direct:

This isn't the place for open-ended or opinion-based questions. For instance, instead of asking, "How do you feel about online banking?", ask, "Do you use online banking?"

3. Limit the Number:

While it might be tempting to have multiple screener questions to get the "perfect" respondent, too many can deter participation. Typically, three to five well-thought-out screeners should suffice.

4. Be Cautious with Demographics:

Questions about age, gender, ethnicity, or other demographics should be handled with sensitivity. Ensure you're asking these questions because they're relevant to the research, not just out of curiosity.

5. Avoid Leading Questions:

We've touched upon this before, but it bears repeating. Leading questions can bias your respondents. Instead of, "You use smartphones frequently, don't you?", opt for, "How often do you use a smartphone?"

6. Test, Test, Test:

Before rolling out your survey, pilot your screener questions. This helps catch any ambiguities or issues that might arise in the larger survey.

Common Pitfalls and How to Avoid Them

a) Double-Barreled Questions:

These are questions that touch upon two subjects but allow for only one answer. For example, "Do you own a car and a house?" Separate these into two distinct questions to get clear answers.

b) Assumptions:

Avoid assuming any knowledge or behavior. "How often do you visit luxury resorts?" presumes the respondent has visited luxury resorts. Instead, first ask if they have, then proceed based on their answer.

c) Vague Terms:

What's "frequent"? Or "seldom"? These terms can mean different things to different people. Be precise in your wording.

Making the Most of Your Screener Data

It might seem like a waste to discard the data from respondents who don't pass the screener. But hold on! This data can give insights into the larger audience landscape. For example, if a large chunk of respondents is excluded due to a particular criterion, it might highlight a trend or an area worth exploring in a separate study.

Shaping the Journey Ahead

Once respondents pass the screener stage, ensure that the subsequent questions align with the criteria set in the screener. It sounds obvious, but it's an oversight that happens. If you've screened for people who use online banking, don't follow up with generic banking questions. Dive deep into their online experiences.

Wrapping It Up: The Gatekeeper's Chronicle

Crafting the right screener questions is like setting the stage for a performance. The stage must be sturdy, the props in place, and the backdrop fitting. Only then can the actors truly shine. Likewise, with the right respondents, your survey can delve into the depths you desire, bringing up pearls of insights.

7 / finding and selecting users

creating participant personas

IMAGINE WALKING into a room filled with vibrant, varied personalities. You see James, the tech-savvy millennial with an adventurous spirit. Sarah, the busy professional juggling her career and raising two kids. Or Raj, the retiree who's become a passionate advocate for sustainable gardening. These aren't just random individuals; they're participant personas, fictional but grounded representatives of your target audience.

The concept of a persona might sound like something straight out of a drama class, but it's become a linchpin in understanding and communicating with target audiences in a variety of industries, especially when crafting comprehensive surveys.

Dive into the Persona Pool

A participant persona, in essence, is a detailed and semi-fictional representation of an ideal survey participant based on real data and some select educated assumptions. The persona encapsulates the needs, goals, and observed behavior patterns of your potential participants. It's like putting a face and story to the data points.

Why Bother with Personas?

You might wonder, "I've got demographics and other data. Why this added layer?" Great question! Personas bring your data to life. They:

1. Provide clarity and focus: It's much easier to design a survey when you have a clear picture of who you're talking to. Would you ask James, the millennial, about his preferences in vinyl records? Probably not. But Raj, the retiree, might have a collection!

2. Facilitate empathy: By understanding the needs and challenges of your personas, you can tailor your questions in a way that resonates with them.

3. Enhance team alignment: Personas offer a shared understanding among team members, ensuring everyone is on the same page about the target audience.

Crafting Your Personas: Where to Begin?

1. Data Collection:

Start with a mix of quantitative (like surveys) and qualitative (like interviews) methods. Remember

Sarah, the busy professional? You might find her in the segment of respondents who work 40+ hours a week and have kids under 10.

2. Spot Patterns:

Look for commonalities and trends in your data. Maybe a significant number of respondents prefer online shopping and are concerned about eco-friendly packaging.

3. Flesh Out the Details:

Once you've identified patterns, start creating a narrative. For instance, if a large segment of your audience is into sustainable practices, imagine a persona who recycles religiously and shops at local farmer's markets.

4. Make it Comprehensive:

Each persona should have:

- Demographics: Age, gender, occupation, etc.

- Behavior patterns: Shopping habits, online behavior, hobbies.

- Motivations: What drives them? It could be saving time, money, the environment, and so on.

- Challenges: What obstacles do they face in achieving their goals?

5. Give Them a Name (and maybe a face!):

It sounds trivial, but naming your persona and even attaching a stock photo makes them memorable and relatable.

6. Refinement:

As with most processes, your personas aren't set in stone. As you gain more insights, revisit and refine them.

A Word of Caution

While personas are immensely helpful, they are, at the end of the day, a generalization. Always be open to the idea that real participants might not fit neatly into your created categories. Also, it's essential not to stereotype. Personas should be based on data and research, not assumptions or biases.

Integrating Personas in Your Survey Design

With your personas in hand, you're better equipped to craft questions that resonate. For example, if one of your personas is a college student with a tight budget, you'd know to include questions about affordability and value for money.

Furthermore, by considering each persona's challenges and motivations, you can tailor your survey's flow and logic. If one persona is less tech-savvy, perhaps you'd opt for simpler question formats and fewer interactive elements.

Taking a Step Back: The Big Picture

Creating participant personas is a bit like assembling a puzzle. Each piece, each data point, contributes to the bigger picture. When done right, they're not just static profiles but dynamic tools that evolve with your understanding of your audience.

In the journey of survey creation, these personas become your trusted companions, guiding your decisions and offering clarity. By understanding the 'who' deeply, you not only ensure that your questions hit the mark but also create a survey experience that's engaging and empathetic.

methods of user recruitment: pros and cons

Ah, user recruitment. It's like casting a wide net into the vast sea of potential participants, hoping to bring in the most suitable catch. Whether you're spearheading a market research project or refining a product's design, getting the right users to provide feedback is half the battle. But how do you rally these individuals? Let's delve into various methods of user recruitment and weigh the pros and cons of each.

1. Direct Outreach

Imagine you're in a café, and you see someone reading a magazine related to your industry. You could simply approach them, introduce your project, and see if they'd be interested, right?

Pros:

- Personal Touch: This method allows you to have a face-to-face interaction, building trust.

- Highly Relevant: Since you're choosing who to approach, you can select individuals who fit your user profile closely.

Cons:

- Time-consuming: This method is labor-intensive and may not yield high numbers quickly.

- Potential for Bias: There's a risk of unconscious bias affecting your choice of whom to approach.

2. Online Advertisements

Think of the many times an ad popped up on your social media feed or a website, inviting you to participate in a study or test a new app.

Pros:

- Wide Reach: Ads can reach a vast number of people across different geographies and demographics.

- Targeted: Modern online ad platforms allow you to fine-tune who sees your ad based on various parameters.

Cons:

- Cost: Running ads, especially on popular platforms, can get expensive.

- Low Conversion: Not everyone who sees your ad might be interested, leading to lower conversion rates.

3. Using Recruitment Agencies

These are the middlemen of the user recruitment world. They maintain databases of potential participants and can quickly find individuals that match your criteria.

Pros:

- Efficient: With their ready databases, agencies can speed up the recruitment process.

- Expertise: They're adept at screening participants, ensuring you get quality respondents.

Cons:

- Expense: Agencies will charge for their services, which could be a significant addition to your budget.

- Less Control: Since you're outsourcing, you have less direct control over the recruitment process.

4. Referral Programs

It's the age-old 'word of mouth' in a structured format. Encourage existing participants or users to refer others who might be suitable.

Pros:

- Trusted Sources: Referrals come from known individuals, increasing the likelihood of quality participants.

- Cost-effective: Often, this method might be cheaper than running extensive ad campaigns or hiring agencies.

Cons:

- Limited Diversity: You might end up with a

homogeneous group, especially if referrals come from tight-knit communities.

- Potential for Misunderstandings: Referrers might not fully understand your requirements, leading to unsuitable referrals.

5. Community Forums and Social Media Groups

Communities, both online and offline, centered around specific interests, can be goldmines for user recruitment.

Pros:

- Targeted Reach: If you're looking for graphic designers, for instance, a design forum might give you a concentrated audience.

- Engagement: Since these users are already engaged in community discussions, they might be more inclined to participate.

Cons:

- Over-saturation: Popular forums might see multiple recruitment posts, making yours just another drop in the ocean.

- Moderation: Some communities have strict rules about recruitment posts and might require permissions or fees.

6. Existing User Base

If you already have a product or service, why not tap into your existing user base for feedback?

Pros:

- Relevance: These users already have experience with your product, making their insights invaluable.
- Ease: You already have a channel of communication with them, be it emails or app notifications.

Cons:

- Bias: Existing users might have preconceived notions or biases based on their past experiences.
- Lack of Fresh Perspectives: New or potential users can offer insights current users might miss.

Alright, with these methods laid out, you might be wondering which one is the "best". And here's the thing: there's no one-size-fits-all answer. The ideal method hinges on your project's specifics, your budget, timeline, and the kind of participants you're aiming for.

When you start recruiting, remember it's a dynamic process. Feel free to mix and match methods, iterate, and adapt based on the results you see. The world of user recruitment is vast and varied, and navigating it effectively requires a blend of strategy, patience, and a dash of creativity.

incentivizing participation without compromising data quality

Picture this: you've just baked a fresh batch of cookies. They're on the counter, cooling, and their tempting aroma wafts through the air. You want to share them, but only with those who can genuinely appreciate the effort you've put into baking. Would you give them away to the first person who walks past your door, or would you prefer they go to someone who loves the art of baking as much as you do?

Such is the challenge of incentivizing participation in research or feedback processes. On one hand, incentives can dramatically boost participation rates. On the other, they can sometimes attract participants who are more interested in the reward than providing genuine feedback. It's a delicate balance, and in this chapter, we'll explore how to strike it.

1. The Double-Edged Sword of Incentives

Incentives, be they monetary, gifts, or other perks, act as a magnet. They can pull in a wide array of participants. But there's always the looming question: Are these participants genuinely interested, or are they here just for the goodies?

To navigate this, it's essential to understand the types of participants you might encounter:

- Genuinely Interested: These participants are intrinsically motivated. They care about your product, service, or research and would probably participate even without incentives.

- Incentive Seekers: These are folks who primarily join for the reward. Their feedback might be hasty or superficial since their main goal is to finish the task and claim their prize.

- The In-betweeners: This group is a mix. They're interested in the incentive but also care enough to provide authentic feedback.

2. Matching Incentives to Goals

The nature and value of the incentive can play a significant role in the type of participant you attract.

Low-value Incentives (e.g., discount coupons, badges):

- Likely to attract a broader audience.
- Risk of reduced data quality as some might rush through the process.

High-value Incentives (e.g., cash rewards, premium products):

- Can attract a dedicated group willing to invest time and effort.
- Risk of attracting those who are only there for the big reward.

Non-monetary Incentives (e.g., feedback on their input, early access to products):

- Attracts genuinely interested participants.
- Lesser risk of compromised data quality, but might result in a smaller pool of participants.

3. Layered Incentives: A Balanced Approach

One way to ensure data quality while using incentives is to employ a layered or tiered approach:

- Initial Participation: Offer a low-value incentive for everyone who completes the survey or feedback process.

- In-depth Feedback: Provide an additional incentive for those who offer more comprehensive feedback or participate in follow-up activities.

- Loyalty Rewards: For those who repeatedly engage in your feedback processes over time, offer cumulative rewards or loyalty bonuses.

4. Quality Checks and Balances

- Pilot Testing: Before rolling out your main survey or feedback process, conduct a small pilot. This will give you a sense of the quality of data you might receive and whether the incentives are skewing the results.

- Randomized Questions: Introduce questions that require careful reading to answer correctly. This can act as a filter, ensuring participants are genuinely engaged.

- Feedback on Feedback: Offer participants insights into how their feedback is being used. Knowing that their input has tangible results can motivate genuine participation.

5. Transparency is Golden

Be upfront about what participants can expect in terms of incentives. If there are conditions to be met or if only a subset of participants will receive the reward, make that clear from the outset. Misunderstandings or feelings of being misled can lead to rushed participation or negative feedback.

6. Feedback Loop

Consider setting up a feedback loop where participants can share their experiences with the feedback process itself. Did they feel the incentive was fair? Were they motivated to give genuine feedback? This meta-feedback can offer valuable insights into refining your incentivization strategy.

Navigating the dance of incentives is indeed a challenge, but when done right, it can lead to a harmonious blend of quality data and satisfied participants. It's about recognizing the value of genuine feedback and ensuring that while participants are rewarded for their time, the primary focus remains on gathering authentic, actionable insights.

8 / deployment strategies for maximum reach

choosing the right platform: from web to email to apps

PICTURE THIS SCENARIO: you've meticulously planned your survey, crafted questions with precision, incentivized participation brilliantly, but now you're at a crossroads. Where do you host your survey? It's a digital era, and the abundance of platforms is both a boon and a dilemma. Web, email, dedicated apps, or perhaps a blend? Let's navigate this together.

1. The Vast Landscape of Web Surveys

Ah, the internet - the vast expanse where most of our modern-day activities take place. Here are some considerations:

- Universality: Web-based surveys are accessible to

anyone with an internet connection. No downloads required, just click on a link and off you go.

- Embedding and Integration: Websites allow you to embed videos, interactive elements, and even chatbots to enhance the survey experience.

- But Remember... Not all web designs are mobile-responsive. If your audience is likely to respond via mobile, ensure your design is adaptable.

2. Email Surveys: Direct and Personal

Imagine getting a personalized invitation in your mailbox. That's what an email survey feels like!

- Direct Reach: Emails land directly in your respondent's inbox. No third-party ads or distractions, just your message.

- Tailored Messaging: Personalize your emails. Use their first name, mention previous interactions, and make them feel valued.

- However... Overzealous spam filters or a cluttered inbox can be a hurdle. Engaging subject lines are crucial, and always give an option to opt-out.

3. Dive Into the World of Apps

Mobile apps are to smartphones what coffee is to mornings. Essential and invigorating!

- Instant Notifications: App-based surveys can utilize push notifications. A little nudge can significantly boost response rates.

- Offline Access: Some apps allow users to take surveys offline, syncing data once they're back online.

- But... App development can be resource-intensive. Moreover, getting a user to download a dedicated survey app might be a tough sell unless it offers substantial value.

4. Mix and Match: A Multi-Platform Approach

Why restrict yourself to one platform? A blended approach can offer the best of all worlds:

- Segment Your Audience: Maybe your younger demographic prefers app-based interactions, while your older respondents are more email-centric. Cater to both!

- Centralized Data Collection: Use tools that allow you to gather data from multiple sources but view it in a unified manner. It'll save you from data juggling later.

5. Key Considerations When Choosing a Platform

- Demographics: A tech-savvy audience might be more receptive to app-based surveys, while a corporate audience might find email more convenient.

- Nature of Survey: Lengthy, in-depth surveys might be better suited for web platforms where respondents can take their time, while quick polls could shine on mobile apps.

- Budget and Resources: Custom app development

is pricey. Off-the-shelf solutions might suffice if you don't need too many bells and whistles.

6. Always Be Adaptable

Technology evolves, and so do user preferences. What's en vogue today might become obsolete tomorrow. It's essential to:

- Stay Updated: Regularly review the platforms you use. Are they still serving your purpose?

- Seek Feedback: At the end of your survey, add a meta-question. How was their experience on the platform they used? This can guide future platform decisions.

Imagine you're hosting a dinner party. You've got the menu down, but where do you serve it? In the living room where everyone's comfortable? The dining room for a touch of formality? Or an outdoor barbecue for a breezy feel? That's precisely what choosing a platform feels like. Each has its flavor, its vibe, and its unique offerings. The key is to match the essence of your survey with the ambiance of the platform.

timing your survey: days, duration, and frequency

It's been said that timing is everything, and when it comes to surveys, this adage holds more truth than you might think. You've chosen your platform and crafted your questions, but now you're pondering, "When's the best moment to launch this into the world?" Let's unravel this puzzle together, shall we?

1. Which Days Are Best?

Weekdays or weekends? Before coffee or after? These are valid questions that might pop up in your head.

- Weekdays: Most professionals check their emails and online portals during the week. For B2B surveys, or any survey targeting working professionals, the midweek – think Tuesday to Thursday – is your sweet spot.

- Weekends: If you're aiming for a younger crowd or a demographic that's typically off-grid during the workweek, weekends can be golden.

- The Monday and Friday Debate: Mondays are often hectic; Fridays, minds wander to weekend plans. Be cautious with these days, but don't discard them outright. They might work, depending on the context and the audience.

2. Time of Day – Hitting the Sweet Spot

Now that we've narrowed down the days, what about the hours?

- Morning Glory: Post-coffee pre-lunch hours, say between 10 am and 11:30 am, can be prime time. The day's chaos hasn't fully erupted, and there's a window of relative calm.

- Afternoon Lull: Post-lunch, between 2 pm and 3 pm, might see a dip in responsiveness. But, late afternoon, as folks wrap up their day, can offer another window, especially around 4 pm.

- Evening and Nights: Unless your target demographic is night owls or folks in a different time zone, it's wise to avoid late-night sends.

3. Duration: How Long Should Your Survey Stay Open?

You've sent out your survey, but how long do you wait for those precious responses?

- Short and Sweet: A week is often standard for many surveys. It provides ample time for respondents to engage without dragging it out unnecessarily.

- Extended Stays: For more in-depth surveys, especially ones requiring thoughtful, qualitative responses, consider a two to three-week window. But keep your audience informed about deadlines.

4. Frequency: Avoiding the Overkill

No one likes that friend who keeps repeating the same story, right? The same goes for surveys.

- One-off Surveys: If it’s a unique survey, say post-event feedback, once is enough.

- Recurring Surveys: For employee engagement or customer satisfaction metrics, quarterly or bi-annually is standard. Monthly can work too but beware of survey fatigue.

- Pulse Checks: Short, quick-fire surveys can be more frequent, even weekly. They're less intrusive and can track real-time sentiments.

5. Reminders: A Nudge, Not a Shove

You've sent your survey, but the responses are trickling in slower than you'd like.

- The Gentle Reminder: A single follow-up email can work wonders. Frame it as a gentle nudge, not a pushy prod.

- The Final Call: If you're nearing the end of your survey window, a last reminder can create a sense of urgency.

But remember, too many reminders can be counterproductive. No one wants to feel pestered.

6. Adapting to Feedback and External Factors

Staying flexible is the name of the game. If a significant event, say a major holiday or news event, coincides with your survey timing, be ready to pivot.

- Adapt and Overcome: If response rates are lower than expected, maybe it's not just the content. Reevaluate your timing strategy.

- Seek Feedback: If recipients are opening but not completing the survey, perhaps ask a few why. Maybe it arrived at a busy time or got lost in a sea of year-end emails.

Imagine a theatre play. Even if the script is exceptional and the actors are top-notch, if the curtains rise at an inopportune time, the seats might be empty. That's what survey timing feels like. It's not just about the content; it's about presenting it at the right moment to the right audience.

a/b testing your survey invitations

Chocolate or vanilla? Beach holiday or mountain retreat? When it comes to survey invitations, the stakes might be higher than choosing ice cream flavors, but the principle remains the same. You want to figure out what works best, and that's where A/B testing swoops in like a knight in shining armor.

1. A Quick Refresher on A/B Testing

At its core, A/B testing, sometimes called split testing, is about comparing two versions of something to figure out which one performs better. In our context, it's about sending two slightly different survey invitations to separate groups within your target audience. By observing which invitation gets a higher response rate, you can optimize for success.

2. Why Bother with A/B Testing?

Well, every percentage point increase in your response rate means more data, more insights, and ultimately, more informed decisions. If a simple tweak can enhance engagement, it's certainly worth the effort!

3. Elements You Can Test

The beauty of A/B testing is its versatility. Let's walk through some of the elements ripe for testing in your survey invitation:

- Subject Lines: This is the first thing your audience sees. A question versus a statement, curiosity-driven versus straightforward, long versus short - there's a world of possibilities here.

- Sender Name: Sometimes, an email from 'The Team at XYZ' feels impersonal compared to one from 'Jane from XYZ'.

- Invitation Tone and Content: Do your respondents prefer a formal tone, or do they engage more with a casual, friendly vibe?

- Visuals: If your email platform allows, test variations in imagery, color schemes, or even button sizes.

- Call to Action (CTA): A 'Take the survey' might not resonate as well as a 'Share your thoughts!'.

4. The Process Simplified

Now, diving into the nuts and bolts:

- Divide and Conquer: Split your audience into two random, equal groups. This ensures both groups are representative of your entire audience.

- Introduce the Variation: Send one version of your invitation to Group A and the different version to Group B.

- Analyze: After a set period, check which version

had a better open rate, click-through rate, and completion rate.

- Implement: Use the winning version for the rest of your audience or in future surveys.

5. Best Practices and Common Pitfalls

While A/B testing sounds straightforward, there are potential traps. Here are some tips and pitfalls to be wary of:

- One at a Time: Test one element at a time. If you modify both the subject line and the CTA, and see a difference in response rates, how will you know which change made the impact?

- Statistical Significance: Ensure your sample size is large enough that the results you see aren't just by chance. There are handy online calculators for this.

- Consistency: Ensure other factors remain consistent. For instance, send both versions of your invitation at the same time to avoid timing biases.

- Document Everything: Record your hypotheses, the changes made, the results, and the decisions taken. This isn't just meticulousness for its own sake; it'll help you refine future tests.

6. Beyond the Open Rate

While the open rate of your survey invitation is crucial, don't forget the end goal: survey completion. A catchy subject line might get someone to open the email, but if they don’t complete the survey, it’s a missed opportunity. Always keep an eye on the completion rate as your primary metric.

7. Continuous Improvement

A/B testing isn't a one-off activity. As you gather more data and insights, revisit your survey invitations. The preferences of your audience might change, and staying attuned to these shifts ensures your surveys remain engaging.

And there we have it! A deep dive into the art and science of A/B testing for survey invitations. Remember, it's all about understanding your audience. While best practices provide a roadmap, every audience is unique. Being open to experimentation and adaptation is the key.

9 / crafting effective follow-up communications

the art of the follow-up email

IMAGINE you're at a networking event. You've just had a riveting conversation with someone who might just be your next business partner, client, or collaborator. You exchange business cards, make promises to connect again... and then the silence descends. The initial excitement fades, and you're left wondering if they remembered you at all. This, my friend, is where the art of the follow-up shines.

1. Why Follow-Up Emails Matter

Follow-up emails are the digital equivalent of that reassuring pat on the shoulder – a gentle reminder that says, "Hey, I remember our conversation, and I value it." When it comes to surveys, follow-up emails play an essential role. They can nudge a respondent who might have forgotten to complete the survey or provide an opportunity to re-engage with someone who showed initial interest.

2. Crafting That Perfect Follow-Up

Here are some elements to consider:

- The Timing: Strike while the iron is hot, but don't burn your chances. Typically, waiting 48 to 72 hours after the initial email strikes a balance between being persistent and respectful.

- Subject Line's Charm: A good follow-up subject line acknowledges the previous communication. Think along the lines of "A quick nudge about our earlier chat," or "Hoping to hear your thoughts soon!"

- Personalize: Generic follow-ups might as well go straight to the junk folder. Address the recipient by name and reference specifics from your last conversation or communication.

- The Content: This isn't a novel, and brevity is your best friend. Reiterate the purpose of your email, provide any necessary context, and close with a clear call to action.

3. Addressing Different Scenarios

Different situations call for distinct approaches:

- Non-responders: "We noticed you haven't had a chance to complete our survey. Your insights are valuable to us. If you need any assistance or have questions, feel free to reach out."

- Partial completions: "Looks like you started sharing your thoughts but didn't finish. If you hit a snag, let us know how we can help. We'd love to hear from you."

- Feedback or issues: "Thank you for reaching out with your concerns. We're working on resolving the issue and appreciate your patience."

4. Keep it Genuine

Nobody likes the person at the party who's clearly working the room, aiming for quantity over quality. Similarly, your follow-up emails should exude sincerity. If you're thanking someone for their time or feedback, mean it. If you're addressing a concern, ensure it's with genuine intent to resolve, not just placate.

5. The Double Opt-In

Let's say you're reaching out to someone more senior or outside your immediate network. The double opt-in involves first checking if they're interested before introducing them to the topic or person in question. This method ensures that they don't feel ambushed and that they have an exit opportunity if they're not interested.

6. Tools and Platforms

While personalized emails are crucial, it doesn't mean crafting each email from scratch. Several platforms allow you to send tailored follow-ups at scale. Tools like Mailchimp, SendGrid, or HubSpot can be valuable allies. They help automate the process while still allowing for personal touches.

7. Know When to Step Back

Ah, the fine line between persistence and annoyance. If after a couple of follow-ups there's still radio silence, it might be time to step back. Being pushy rarely results in positive engagement.

8. Measure, Adapt, and Refine

Just as with your initial emails, monitor the performance of your follow-ups. Are they being opened? Are they leading to increased engagement? Gathering this data helps you refine your approach, ensuring your follow-ups resonate with the recipients.

There we are! The delicate dance of the follow-up email, unraveled. Remember, at its core, a follow-up is about expressing value and respect for the other party. As we journey further into the world of engagement and communication, it's these small gestures that often make the biggest difference.

strategies to increase response rates

The elusive white whale for many professionals. You've crafted a masterful survey, laid out every detail, and sent it into the digital sea. Now, you wait, hoping for those valuable insights to come pouring in. But what if the silence stretches? What if Moby Dick eludes your grasp?

Never fear. Here are some proven strategies to boost those response rates and ensure your survey doesn't sink into obscurity.

1. The Seductive Power of the Subject Line

A catchy subject line is like a siren's song—it draws people in. Make it intriguing, relevant, and clear. Instead of "Survey Invitation," how about "Help Us Shape the Future of XYZ"?

2. Timing is Everything

Let's face it: a survey invitation on a Monday morning might be overlooked, while one on a Wednesday afternoon might find more success. Some studies suggest Tuesdays and Thursdays have higher open rates. However, know your audience. If you're targeting teachers, for example, weekends or holiday periods might be more apt.

3. A Personal Touch

Everyone likes to feel special. Instead of mass emails, address your potential respondents by name. It might sound like a mammoth task, but with modern tools, it's easier than ever. Personalization goes beyond the name, though. Tailor your content to resonate with the receiver.

4. Keep It Short and Sweet

Ever opened a mail, seen a wall of text, and

instantly hit delete? Yup, we've all been there. Long surveys are intimidating. Let respondents know upfront about the estimated time of completion. And if it's a short one, even better! Make it a selling point.

5. Incentivize, But Wisely

Everyone loves a perk. Offer an incentive, whether it's a discount, an entry into a lucky draw, or an exclusive piece of content. However, be cautious. You want genuine responses, not hasty clicks lured just by the prize.

6. Mobile Optimization

We're living in the age of smartphones, where everything happens on the go. If your survey isn't mobile-friendly, you're missing out on a massive chunk of potential respondents. Ensure it looks good and works seamlessly across devices.

7. A Sneak Peek Can Help

Consider providing a brief overview of the topics covered in the survey. It sets clear expectations and can pique the interest of those who find the subject matter compelling.

8. Send Gentle Reminders

If a respondent hasn't completed the survey, a gentle reminder can work wonders. But remember, there's a thin line between a nudge and a push. Overdoing it might land you in the dreaded spam folder.

9. Social Proof and Credibility

Sometimes, people need to know that others are also participating. Statements like "Join hundreds of your peers..." or showcasing testimonials from past respondents can boost trust and interest.

10. Transparency is Key

Let participants know why you're conducting the survey and how their data will be used. In an age where data privacy is paramount, transparency can be a decisive factor in participation.

11. The Gratitude Gesture

Once a respondent has completed the survey, don't let the conversation end. Thank them for their time, perhaps with a personalized note. This not only leaves a positive impression but might also make them more likely to participate in future surveys.

12. Engage Through Different Channels

Don't restrict yourself to emails. Depending on your target audience, platforms like social media, messaging apps, or even offline methods can be effective. Explore multi-channel engagement to cast a wider net.

13. Iterate and Adapt

Finally, always be prepared to tweak your approach. What worked once might not work again. Collect feedback, assess response patterns, and refine your strategy for the next round.

With these strategies in your arsenal, increasing

response rates is no longer akin to chasing the white whale. It's about creating a symphony of tactics that work harmoniously, ensuring your survey doesn't just float, but sails triumphantly across the vast digital ocean.

addressing non-responses and dropouts

There you are, sipping your morning coffee and analyzing your survey results, when a glaring statistic leaps off the screen: the number of non-responses and dropouts. It's like hosting a party where half the guests didn't show up, and some left before dessert. Frustrating, isn't it?

Non-responses and dropouts are the party-poopers of the survey world, but with the right strategies, they're not insurmountable challenges. Let's dive into the why's, the what's, and most importantly, the how-to's of tackling this issue.

Understanding the Root Cause

The first step in addressing any problem is understanding its root cause. There could be a myriad of reasons why someone didn't complete your survey:

- Survey Length: Perhaps they underestimated the time commitment and had to abandon ship halfway through.

- Complex Questions: Maybe a particular question was too complicated or required too much introspection.

- Technical Glitches: Nothing deters a respondent faster than a survey that refuses to load or crashes mid-way.

Building Bridges, Not Walls

Once you've identified potential stumbling blocks, you can proactively bridge these gaps:

- Mid-Survey Save Option: Allow respondents to save their progress and return later. This can be particularly useful for longer surveys.

- Simplify: Review your questions. Are there any that are too long-winded or complex? Simplify them without diluting their essence.

- Test for Tech Issues: Before launching your survey, test it on different devices and browsers to ensure there are no glitches.

Re-Engage with Dropouts

When someone exits your survey prematurely, it's a missed opportunity. But all's not lost! Here's how to woo them back:

- Follow Up with a Reminder: A gentle reminder, especially if personalized, can nudge them to complete the survey. Mention any changes you've made based on feedback to show you're actively improving.

- Offer Incentives: If they were on the fence about

completing the survey, a little incentive might tip the balance in your favor.

- Seek Feedback on the Dropout: Sometimes, the best insights come from those who didn't complete the task. Ask them why they didn't finish. Their feedback can be invaluable for future surveys.

The Non-Response Dilemma

Non-responses are trickier than dropouts. If someone hasn't even opened your survey, how do you get them on board?

- Revise Your Invitation: If the initial invite didn’t entice them, maybe it's time for a new approach. Spice up the subject line, or offer a clearer value proposition in the email body.

- Change the Channel: If email isn't working, consider reaching out via social media, SMS, or even a phone call, depending on the context and relationship.

- Time it Right: Just as you wouldn’t call someone at 3 AM, avoid sending surveys at inopportune times. Depending on your audience, adjust the timing of your outreach.

The Bright Side of Non-responses and Dropouts

Wait, is there really a silver lining here? Absolutely! While it's easy to see non-responses and dropouts as failures, they also offer a rich avenue for growth:

- Quality Over Quantity: Sometimes, non-responses

filter out those who aren't genuinely interested, leaving you with more invested respondents.

- Feedback Goldmine: As mentioned earlier, understanding why someone dropped out can provide valuable insights to improve future outreach.

- Set Realistic Expectations: Remember, a 100% response rate is like a unicorn - lovely to imagine, but highly elusive. Strive for improvement, not perfection.

Addressing non-responses and dropouts might feel like chasing a moving target, but with perseverance and adaptability, you can steadily increase engagement. Consider each iteration of your survey as a learning experience, a step closer to crafting the ultimate, irresistible questionnaire.

10 / analyzing and interpreting survey results

cleaning and pre-processing data

AH, the exhilarating thrill of collecting raw data! It's akin to a miner pulling a shimmering stone from the earth, gleaming with potential. But just as that miner knows the gem requires cutting and polishing to reveal its true beauty, you, too, must understand the art and science of refining your data. The process of cleaning and pre-processing is your chisel and cloth, ensuring the insights you draw are both accurate and meaningful.

Why Bother with Data Cleaning?

• • •

Imagine preparing a delicious, intricate dish using a few questionable ingredients. Even if just one component isn't up to par, the entire dish could be compromised. The same goes for your dataset. Dirty or unprocessed data can lead to skewed results, misinformed decisions, and, honestly, a lot of unnecessary confusion.

Spotting the Culprits

Let's start by identifying common data contaminants:

- Duplicates: These are the echo in the data chorus, repeating values that can inflate results.
- Missing Values: The enigmatic blanks that leave gaps in our understanding.
- Outliers: Those wild, far-off data points that skew averages and other measures.
- Inconsistencies: A mishmash of formats, units, or even typos that can lead to categorization errors.

Rolling Up Those Sleeves: The Cleaning Process

• • •

1. Duplicates Begone!

Use tools or software that can identify and eliminate duplicate entries. Remember to cross-check, though. Sometimes what looks like a duplicate could be valid repeated data.

2. Addressing the Void:

Missing values are tricky. You can:

- Delete: If the missing value won't significantly impact your dataset, removing that entry might be the simplest solution.

- Impute: Fill in the blanks based on other available data. Mean, median, or mode are popular choices, but more sophisticated techniques like regression can also be employed.

- Flag and Move On: In some cases, it might be worth keeping the missing value, marking it clearly, and analyzing it separately.

3. The Outliers' Ball:

Outliers aren't necessarily bad. They might be genuine anomalies worth investigating. However, when they distort the general trend, consider:

. . .

- Capping: Limit the extreme values to a predetermined threshold.

- Transformation: Using mathematical methods like logarithms to compress the scale.

- Separate Analysis: Study outliers independently to understand their nature.

4. Consistency is Key:

Ensure your data speaks the same language. This means:

- Standardizing Units: If half your data is in kilograms and the other half in pounds, pick one.

- Format Uniformity: Dates, for instance, should follow a consistent format, be it MM-DD-YYYY or DD-MM-YYYY.

- Spellcheck and Validation: Especially in manually entered data, watch out for typos or variations in naming conventions.

Pre-processing: Setting the Stage

. . .

Once the data is clean, it's time to prepare it for analysis. This can involve:

- Feature Selection: Identify which data columns or variables are most relevant to your analysis.
- Normalization: Especially in datasets with varying scales, this step ensures all data is on a comparable scale.
- Encoding: Transform categorical data (like 'yes' or 'no' responses) into numerical values, so they're ready for statistical analysis.

Tools of the Trade

While one can clean and pre-process data manually, especially in smaller datasets, several tools can make the job much smoother. Software solutions like Excel, Python libraries such as Pandas, and specialized platforms like Alteryx or Talend, can expedite the process while reducing the margin for human error.

Parting Thoughts

• • •

While it might be tempting to dive directly into analysis after collecting data, this intermediary step of cleaning and pre-processing is essential. It's akin to tuning an instrument before a concert. The effort you put into these stages ensures the final performance — or in this case, the final analysis — is pitch-perfect.

quantitative analysis techniques for survey data

You've meticulously collected your data, refined it with tender care, and now stand at the precipice of the treasure trove of insights it promises. Welcome to the world of quantitative analysis, where numbers dance to the rhythm of logic, patterns emerge, and the story behind every survey unfolds.

Why Quantitative Analysis Matters

Ever found yourself lost in thought, gazing at a starry night? Each star might seem similar from afar, but on closer examination, every single one has its own tale to tell. Similarly, every respondent in your survey has shared a piece of their narrative. Quantitative analysis is the telescope that helps you discern the constellations in this sky of data.

Starting Simple: Descriptive Statistics

Before delving deep, it's essential to get a feel of the data's pulse. Enter descriptive statistics:

- Frequency Distribution: Essentially, how often does each response appear? It's a headcount of sorts for your answers.

- Measures of Central Tendency: The big trio - mean (average), median (middle value), and mode (most frequent value) - offers a snapshot of where the bulk of your responses lie.

- Dispersion Measures: The range, variance, and standard deviation tell you how spread out your data is. Are the responses huddled close together or spread far and wide?

• • •

Diving Deeper: Inferential Statistics

While descriptive statistics provide an overview, inferential statistics help you, well, infer and draw conclusions:

- T-Tests: Suppose you're curious if men and women have different opinions based on your survey. A t-test will help you determine if the difference in their average responses is statistically significant.

- ANOVA (Analysis of Variance): It's like the t-test's big sibling. When comparing more than two groups, ANOVA steps in to ascertain if there are significant differences between their means.

- Regression Analysis: Want to predict one variable based on another? For instance, does the number of hours someone works predict their job satisfaction score? Regression can help!

The Power of Cross-tabulation

• • •

Imagine slicing your data cake from multiple angles to see the various layers. Cross-tabulation, often accompanied by chi-square tests, allows you to examine relationships between different survey questions. If 90% of people who answered 'Yes' to owning a pet also reported higher happiness scores, you might be onto something!

Visual Aids: Charting It Out

A well-placed graph can speak volumes:

- Bar and Column Charts: Great for comparing different categories or seeing changes over a short time.

- Histograms: If you want to look at frequency distributions, histograms are your best buddies.

• • •

- Pie Charts: Want a percentage breakdown of responses for a particular question? Slice up that data pie!

- Scatter Plots: Ideal for spotting trends or patterns between two variables.

Correlation Does Not Mean Causation

A quick pit stop for a word of caution. You might find two variables moving in tandem, but remember, that doesn't automatically mean one causes the other. Always approach such findings with a critical mind and explore potential external factors.

The Role of Software

While the thought of calculating standard deviations or running regressions might sound daunting, fear not! Software platforms, from SPSS to Excel, are equipped with tools to make quantitative analysis a breeze. It's like having a friendly math wizard by your side, guiding you through the maze of numbers.

Wrapping Up: Revel in the Discovery

Embarking on the journey of quantitative analysis is akin to setting off on an exploration. There will be moments of wonder, times of confusion, and occasional frustrations. But, oh, the exhilaration when patterns emerge, narratives form, and insights dawn!

interpreting qualitative responses: thematic analysis and coding

Dive into the sea of qualitative data, and you might initially feel like you're swimming amidst a school of fish with no discernible direction. Every respondent provides a unique perspective, but how do you make sense of these myriad voices and narratives? Welcome to the realm of thematic analysis and coding—a compass to navigate the vast ocean of words and find the treasure of insights buried within.

Why Qualitative Data Deserves Love

. . .

While quantitative data gives you the numbers, qualitative data provides the stories, emotions, and nuances. Think of it as the difference between knowing that 70% of respondents prefer chocolate ice cream and understanding why they have this preference. Perhaps it reminds them of childhood summers, or maybe there's an irresistible richness to chocolate they can't resist.

Unraveling Thematic Analysis

At its core, thematic analysis is about identifying, analyzing, and interpreting patterns (themes) within qualitative data. It's like piecing together a jigsaw puzzle where each response is a unique piece, and themes are the bigger picture they collectively create.

1. Familiarizing Yourself with the Data: Dive in, read, and re-read the responses. Absorb them. This stage is all about immersion.

. . .

2. Generating Initial Codes: As you sift through the data, certain patterns, ideas, or keywords will begin to emerge. Label or "code" these.

3. Searching for Themes: Group these codes together. What overarching ideas do they present? These clusters become your themes.

4. Reviewing Themes: Do the themes make sense? Are there overlaps, or perhaps a theme that's too broad or too narrow? Refinement is key here.

5. Defining and Naming Themes: What does each theme represent? Giving it a succinct, descriptive name can make interpretation easier.

6. Writing the Analysis: With your themes in hand, it's time to describe and explore them, discussing their nuances, significance, and the story they tell.

Coding: Not Just for Computers

• • •

Coding isn't about turning humans into binaries. It's a system of labeling responses to make sense of them systematically. Every time a respondent mentions "nostalgia" when talking about chocolate ice cream, that's a code. Over time, these codes help unveil the broader themes.

1. Open Coding: Start without any predefined structure. Let the data guide you and code freely.

2. Axial Coding: Here, you begin to see how codes relate to one another. It's a process of connection and refinement.

3. Selective Coding: At this stage, you're pinpointing the central theme that runs through your data, a sort of "core" theme, if you will.

Ensuring Reliability in Your Analysis

While qualitative analysis involves interpretation, it shouldn’t be akin to reading tea leaves. Having a colleague or team member independently analyze a subset of the data can be beneficial. If both of you identify similar themes, that's a reassuring nod to the reliability of the analysis.

The Delicate Balance of Subjectivity and Objectivity

It's true; qualitative analysis does have a subjective element. After all, you're interpreting human emotions and experiences. However, always approach the data with an open mind. Preconceptions or biases have no place here. Your job is to listen to the data, not dictate it.

Embracing the Power of Software

We live in a digital age, and thematic analysis is no exception. Tools like NVivo or Atlas.ti have been designed to make qualitative data analysis more streamlined and systematic. They can help in coding, visualizing data, and ensuring nothing gets overlooked.

• • •

The Stories That Emerge

When you've meticulously moved through the steps of thematic analysis and coding, a moment of revelation awaits. From seemingly disparate responses emerges a tapestry of narratives, emotions, and insights. The qualitative data sings its song, a melody composed of countless individual notes.

visualizing your findings: best practices

Think of it as the translation of your meticulous analysis into a universally comprehensible language. Where words may falter or become verbose, a well-crafted chart or graph can communicate volumes. But how do we ensure that our visual representations are not just attractive but also accurate and insightful? Let's embark on this colorful journey together.

Why Visuals Matter

Imagine being handed a dense, 50-page report brimming with numbers, text, and statistics. It's intimidating, isn't it? Now, juxtapose this with a report interspersed with vibrant charts, graphs, and infographics. The difference is palpable. Visuals break the monotony, simplify complex data, and make your findings accessible to a wider audience.

The Cardinal Rules of Data Visualization

1. Simplicity is the Ultimate Sophistication: Your goal isn't to dazzle with intricate designs but to communicate effectively. Sometimes, a straightforward bar chart can be more powerful than a complex 3D graph.

2. Maintain Data Integrity: It's easy to manipulate visuals to suit a narrative. Avoid this temptation. The scale, proportions, and representation should always uphold the data's authenticity.

3. Color Wisely: Colors can evoke emotions and highlight data. But overdoing it can be distracting. Stick to a consistent palette and ensure it's accessible even for those with color vision deficiencies.

• • •

Choosing the Right Visualization

The type of visualization largely depends on the nature of your data and the story you want to convey:

1. Bar and Column Charts: Ideal for comparing data across categories. For example, survey responses from different age groups.

2. Pie Charts: Suitable for depicting parts of a whole. However, use with caution—too many segments can lead to confusion.

3. Line Graphs: Perfect for tracking changes or trends over periods.

4. Heat Maps: They highlight data magnitude using colors. Imagine showcasing response concentration across different regions.

• • •

5. Scatter Plots: If you're trying to find a relationship between two variables, this is your go-to graph.

The Fine Art of Annotation

Providing context can be the difference between a vague and a compelling visualization. Annotations, labels, and legends offer additional insights without overwhelming the main visual.

Interactivity: The Modern Touch

With tools like Tableau or Power BI, you can make your visualizations interactive. This means the audience isn't just passively absorbing but actively engaging with the data. They can zoom, filter, or even ask questions—making the experience immersive.

Testing and Feedback

. . .

Before finalizing, gather feedback. Show your visualizations to colleagues, preferably those not deeply involved in the project. Their fresh perspective can help you identify areas of confusion or potential improvement.

Adapting Visuals for Different Mediums

A visual that looks stellar on a desktop might not translate as well on a mobile device or in print. Ensure that your visuals are adaptable across different mediums. This might mean creating different versions or ensuring that interactive elements degrade gracefully.

Storytelling Through Visualization

Data tells a story, and your visualizations are the narrative tools. Sequence them logically, highlight the key moments, and guide your audience through the journey. A well-structured story can captivate even the most data-averse person.

• • •

Avoiding Common Pitfalls

- Too Much Data: Overloading a single visualization can make it unreadable. Spread out your data if needed.

- Inconsistent Scales: Always ensure that the scales across graphs or within a graph remain consistent unless there's a valid reason for changing them.

- Overdesign: Aesthetic appeal is essential, but never at the cost of clarity. Avoid unnecessary decorations or graphics.

Continual Learning

Data visualization, as a field, is continually evolving. Stay updated with the latest trends, tools, and best practices. This isn't just about making prettier visuals but enhancing the clarity and impact of your communication.

11 / taking action: from insights to design

prioritizing feedback and identifying patterns

IT'S AS diverse and varied as a bustling marketplace. You'll find gems of insight, occasional pieces of irrelevant chatter, and sometimes a chorus of voices pointing towards a glaring oversight. The question that often looms large is - how do you sift through it all? How do you discern the patterns, the repeated melodies amidst the cacophony? Let's embark on this journey of decoding feedback together.

The Power of Feedback

Feedback, when looked at with the right lens, can be a transformative tool. It can highlight what's working, point out what's not, and even give direction on what could be. But like any tool, its efficacy lies in how you wield it.

The Bucket Approach

A useful way to begin is by imagining you have several buckets in front of you, each labeled with a different category:

1. Usability Concerns: Feedback related to how easy (or challenging) users find to navigate or use your platform or product.

2. Content Queries: Concerns or suggestions related to the material or information you're presenting.

3. Technical Glitches: Issues related to the functionality, bugs, or other technical aspects.

4. General Impressions: Overall sentiments, feelings, or thoughts about your offering.

When you review feedback, assign each piece to one of these buckets. Over time, the fuller buckets can guide you to areas that might need more immediate attention.

Frequency vs. Severity

Not all feedback carries the same weight. Sometimes, an issue that's raised frequently might not be as critical as an issue raised once but has severe implications.

For instance, many users might comment on a color scheme they find unappealing (frequency), but a single user pointing out a data breach (severity) clearly overshadows the former in terms of urgency.

The Art of Pattern Recognition

Identifying patterns is less about quantity and more about quality. Sometimes, even if a piece of feedback is unique, the underlying sentiment might align with broader trends. Let's say only a handful of users comment on the "clunkiness" of your platform. Still, several others mention difficulties in navigating it swiftly. Though the feedback is different, the pattern—usability issues—is consistent.

The Gold in Outliers

Feedback that stands out, that doesn't fit into any of your predefined buckets, is crucial. These are your outliers. They could be pointing towards an aspect you haven't considered, or they might be early indicators of an emerging trend.

Engaging with Feedback Givers

When in doubt, reach out. If you're unsure about certain feedback or need more clarity, consider engaging directly with the person who provided it. Their expanded perspective might shed more light on the issue and even offer potential solutions.

Feedback Workshops

Gather your team and periodically dive deep into the feedback pool. Brainstorm, discuss, debate. These sessions can be invaluable in not just understanding feedback but also in fostering a culture that values it.

Document and Evolve

Maintain a dynamic feedback document. It's not just about listing out the feedback, but also noting down your interpretations, actions taken, and the results of those actions. Over time, this document will become a goldmine of insights, learnings, and growth pathways.

Embrace the Positives

Often, we're so focused on what needs fixing that we overlook what's working. Celebrate the positive feedback. It’s a testament to your team's hard work and can be a morale booster in a feedback-heavy environment.

The Balance of Reactivity and Proactivity

While it's essential to be reactive to feedback, it's equally crucial to be proactive. Use feedback as a compass, not just a map. Let it guide your direction, but chart your path.

Remember, feedback is like a river, ever-flowing and ever-changing. If you stand still, you might get overwhelmed. But if you learn to navigate its currents, you can harness its power to carve out beautiful landscapes.

translating survey findings into design improvements

Imagine you're an archaeologist, and after days of sifting through sand and grit, you've finally unearthed a trove of ancient artifacts. Your survey data is somewhat similar – a treasure trove of insights, waiting to be deciphered. But how do you take these findings and seamlessly weave them into your design tapestry? Let's embark on this transformative journey together.

From Raw Data to Refined Insights

Much like uncut diamonds need a master jeweler's touch to shine, raw survey data requires a keen analytical mind. First off, categorize your findings:

1. Functional Feedback: Concerns related to usability, features, and accessibility.

2. Aesthetic Feedback: Insights on visuals, colors, typography, and overall design elements.

3. Content Feedback: Thoughts on information clarity, relevance, and structuring.

4. Emotional Feedback: Reactions about the overall experience, trustworthiness, and feelings evoked.

Grouping your feedback helps you address each design dimension more effectively.

Decoding the Silent Majority

Not every participant voices their opinion, and yet, their behavior on your platform speaks volumes. Did a significant number abandon a process mid-way? Or did they linger on a page longer than usual? These behavioral clues can help identify design elements that need tweaking.

Prioritize by Impact

Every piece of feedback is valuable, but not all have the same impact. Create a matrix mapping the feedback based on its potential impact on user experience versus the effort required to implement the change. High impact and low effort changes? Those are your low-hanging fruits. Start there.

Sketching the Blueprint

Now, this is where the magic begins. With your refined insights in hand, start creating wireframes or rough sketches to incorporate these changes. These sketches act as a foundation, ensuring everyone's on the same page (pun slightly intended).

Collaborative Iteration

It's brainstorm time! Rally your design and development team and iterate over these wireframes. Their expertise will help translate user feedback into feasible design improvements.

Prototyping and Usability Testing

Once you've agreed upon the changes, develop a prototype. It's like a dress rehearsal for your final product. Conduct usability tests on this prototype, ensuring the changes resonate with the users and actually enhance their experience.

Realigning with Brand Identity

While user feedback is paramount, it's equally important to ensure the design changes align with your brand identity. The last thing you want is a patchwork quilt of design elements that don't harmonize. So, step back and look at the bigger picture. Do these changes feel organic to your brand?

Communicate Changes

When rolling out design improvements, transparency is key. Consider creating a changelog or an update note for your users. Let them know that their feedback was instrumental in shaping these changes. It's not just a courtesy; it fosters trust and a sense of community.

Rinse and Repeat

Design, much like every other discipline, is evolutionary. Today's perfect design could be tomorrow's relic. So, once you've made your changes, it's back to the drawing board - solicit feedback, analyze, and iterate. Keep the cycle going.

Now, let's take a pause and appreciate the journey. It began with raw, unfiltered feedback, almost overwhelming in its magnitude. And yet, with a systematic approach, this feedback became the north star guiding your design enhancements. It's a dance of sorts, between what users desire and what designers envision. And like any dance, it requires grace, rhythm, and a deep connection with your partner, the user.

communicating findings to stakeholders

That elation when you unearth pivotal insights from your data? Oh, the excitement is palpable! But hold onto that metaphorical fedora, Indiana Jones, because the real adventure starts now. Sharing these findings with stakeholders is a nuanced dance, a balancing act between thoroughness and conciseness. Let's dive into how you can make this dance graceful and memorable.

Understanding Stakeholder Persona

First and foremost, know your audience. Stakeholders range from C-level executives with a bird's eye view to project managers knee-deep in the details. Tailoring your message to resonate with their specific concerns and perspectives is half the battle won.

1. Executives: They typically appreciate the big picture. What are the overarching insights, and how do they affect the company's direction or bottom line?

2. Managers: They're your bridge. They need a blend of high-level insights and some details, as they'll be responsible for actioning changes.

3. Technical Teams: They're all about the nitty-

gritty. What are the specifics? How will this affect the systems or processes in place?

Storyboard Your Findings

Let's harness the power of narratives. Organize your findings like you would a story, with a clear beginning, middle, and end. Start with the context or background, delve into the core insights, and end with recommendations or next steps.

Data Visualization: A Picture's Worth a Thousand Numbers

Graphs, charts, and infographics aren't just pretty accessories. They condense complex data into digestible visuals. However, ensure your visual aids align with the story you're weaving. A misplaced or overly complex visual can muddle your narrative rather than clarify it.

Clarity over Complexity

It's easy to get lost in the sea of data and jargon. But for your stakeholders, simplicity reigns supreme. This isn't about dumbing things down; it's about presenting your insights in a way that's instantly graspable. Precision, paired with simplicity, makes for compelling communication.

Anticipate Questions and Concerns

Being proactive can save you a world of back-and-forths later. Think about potential questions stakeholders might have and address them in your presentation. Not only does this demonstrate thoroughness, but it also shows empathy – you're in tune with their concerns.

Interactive Sessions vs. Reports

Reports are fantastic for detailed insights, but interactive sessions (like workshops or presentations) allow for real-time feedback and clarifications. It's often beneficial to pair both – an interactive session backed up by a comprehensive report for stakeholders to peruse at leisure.

The Feedback Loop

Once you've communicated your findings, it's not the end. Encourage feedback. This collaborative approach ensures that stakeholders feel involved and can offer valuable input from their unique perspectives. Remember, insights are not static; they evolve with discussion and collaboration.

Document Everything

While oral presentations have their charm, always back them up with written documentation. This serves as a reference point and ensures that no insight gets lost or misinterpreted. Platforms like shared documents or collaboration tools can be particularly useful here, allowing for real-time updates and comments.

The Empathy Angle

Lastly, but most importantly, infuse your communication with empathy. Behind every data point is a user, a human being. Highlighting the human side of your insights can make them resonate more deeply with stakeholders. It's not just about numbers; it's about experiences, frustrations, and joys.

Navigating through this process might seem a tad overwhelming at first glance. But think of it as a conversation. You've learned something valuable, and now you're sharing it with a group of interested listeners. The medium might vary, the depth of detail might fluctuate, but at its heart, it's a dialogue. And like any good conversation, it's built on clarity, empathy, and mutual respect.

But before we wrap up, let's circle back to our adventure metaphor. If you think about it, presenting your findings is a bit like the climax of a treasure hunt movie. The quest (data analysis) is over, and now, in the grand hall (boardroom or meeting room), you're unveiling the treasures (insights). The stakeholders (audience or, if you will, fellow adventurers) await in anticipation. It's your moment, the spotlight is on, and the room's energy is palpable.

12 / ethical considerations and privacy

ensuring informed consent and transparency

AH, transparency and consent – two words that can seem daunting in the fast-paced world of data collection and analytics. But, before you imagine a dreary landscape of legal jargon and fine print, let's shift our perspective a bit. Think of these principles as the sturdy bridges that connect you to your audience. They're essential in building trust, showing respect, and, quite frankly, keeping things above board.

Diving into Informed Consent

• • •

Picture this: you're at a magician's show, and the magician asks for a volunteer to step up for the next act. Now, wouldn't you want to know what you're getting into before you raise your hand? Similarly, when participants offer their information, they deserve a clear picture of what they're signing up for.

1. Simplicity is Key: While it might be tempting to wrap everything up in professional-sounding language, it's essential to keep things simple. Your participants should understand what you're saying without needing a dictionary or a law degree.

2. What, How, and Why: Clearly lay out what data you're collecting, how you'll use it, and why you need it. If you're using it for research today but might sell it tomorrow, let them know.

3. Risks and Benefits: If there are any potential risks to participants, no matter how small, they should be informed. Likewise, highlight the benefits – not just to you, but to them and the wider community.

The Art of Being Transparent

• • •

In the age of data breaches and privacy concerns, being transparent isn't just good manners – it's a necessity. But how do you ensure transparency without overwhelming your participants with information?

1. Continuous Communication: Instead of a one-time disclosure, consider continuous updates. If the way you use data changes, let your participants know. If you have a significant breakthrough thanks to their data, share the joy.

2. Accessibility: Make sure that any agreements, terms, or data usage policies are easily accessible. A hidden policy is a non-transparent one.

3. Openness to Queries: Create a channel where participants can ask questions or voice concerns. And when they do, respond promptly and sincerely.

When Things Go South: Handling Breaches and Mistakes

It's the situation everyone dreads: something goes wrong. Maybe there was a data breach, or perhaps data was used in a way participants weren't informed about. While these situations are challenging, they're not insurmountable.

1. Prompt Disclosure: The moment you realize there's been a breach or mistake, inform your participants. It's tempting to hide or downplay such incidents, but honesty is crucial here.

2. Action Plan: Clearly outline the steps you're taking to rectify the situation and ensure it doesn't happen again.

3. Apology: Sometimes, a sincere apology can go a long way. Recognize the inconvenience or distress you might have caused and offer a genuine apology.

Evolving Landscape: Staying Updated

Laws and best practices related to data privacy and consent are constantly evolving. It's important to stay updated, not just for compliance but to ensure you're offering the best to your participants.

• • •

1. Regular Training: Whether it's GDPR, CCPA, or the next big data protection regulation, ensure that your team is regularly trained and updated.

2. Feedback Mechanisms: Allow participants to give feedback on your consent and transparency practices. Sometimes, the most valuable insights come from those on the other side.

We began our journey with the image of a sturdy bridge, and as we near the end, let's revisit it. This bridge, built on the pillars of consent and transparency, leads to a land of trust. Trust from your participants, stakeholders, and the wider community. And in a world teeming with data skepticism, that trust is golden.

handling personal data responsibly

We've meandered through the alleys of informed consent and transparency, and now we've arrived at the bustling market square of personal data responsibility. It's a place humming with potential, but like any market square, there's a code of ethics to follow. Dive in, and let's explore how to handle the goldmine of personal data with the respect and responsibility it demands.

. . .

The Why Behind the What

Remember that time when you were entrusted with your friend's secret recipe? You felt honored, didn't you? The act of sharing personal data is no different. When someone shares their personal information with you, they're entrusting you with a part of their identity. Recognizing this is the first step toward understanding the weight of responsibility you carry.

Keeping It Safe

Alright, first things first: Protection. It's akin to storing that secret recipe in a safe place where coffee spills and prying eyes can't reach it.

1. Encryption: Think of encryption as the magic cloak of the digital world. It renders data unreadable to anyone without the decryption key. Ensure that data, both at rest and in transit, is encrypted.

2. Regular Audits: Schedule periodic security audits. Just as you'd check your home's locks now and

then, ensure your data protection mechanisms are always in top shape.

3. Limit Access: Not everyone in your organization needs access to all data. Have clear policies about who can access what. The fewer the hands, the safer the data.

Data Minimization

Sometimes, less truly is more. Collect only what you need. Holding onto unnecessary data not only increases risks but also complicates data management.

1. Review Regularly: Make it a habit to review the data you're collecting. Ask yourself, "Do I really need this?" If the answer isn't a resounding yes, maybe it's time to reconsider.

2. Clear Retention Policies: How long do you hold onto the data? Set clear timelines and stick to them. When the data has served its purpose, ensure it's disposed of safely.

Anonymize and Pseudonymize

• • •

There are times when you don't need to know who the data belongs to, just the patterns and trends it reveals. That's where these techniques come in:

1. Anonymization: This is the process of stripping data of identifiable features. Once anonymized, it's nearly impossible to trace it back to an individual.

2. Pseudonymization: This involves replacing private identifiers with fake ones or pseudonyms. It's reversible, unlike anonymization, provided you have the right key.

Being Accountable

Accountability isn't just about owning up when things go south (though that's a crucial part); it's about being proactive in ensuring data responsibility.

1. Documentation: Maintain clear records of how personal data is being processed and stored. This not

only helps in audits but also instills a sense of discipline.

2. Data Protection Officers: Consider having a dedicated individual or team overseeing data protection. Their sole focus? Ensuring data is handled responsibly.

3. Impact Assessments: Before launching a new project or using data in a new way, assess the potential privacy impacts. Being foresighted can save a lot of trouble down the line.

I bet you've sensed a recurring theme here: Trust. Personal data responsibility isn't just about following laws and best practices (though, of course, that's vital). It's about honoring the trust placed in you. It's about understanding that behind every data point, every click, every response, there's a human being.

addressing biases and promoting inclusivity

You've been doing a terrific job navigating the intricacies of survey research. Having secured personal data responsibly and communicated findings diligently, we're now diving into the realm where numbers meet nuance: the human psyche. Here, biases lurk, often unbeknownst to even the most well-intentioned researcher. But the very fabric of good research is ensuring it represents all voices and not just echoes of the loudest or most privileged. So, let's chat about biases and inclusivity, shall we?

Understanding the Roots of Bias

Biases are sneaky. Sometimes, they're as overt as a billboard and at other times, as subtle as a whisper. But to address them, one must first acknowledge their existence.

1. Cultural Bias: When a survey leans heavily towards the cultural norms and values of one group, it can unintentionally alienate others.

2. Confirmation Bias: Ah, the trap of seeing only what we want to see. Confirmation bias occurs when we favor information that aligns with our existing beliefs.

3. Sampling Bias: This happens when some members of the intended population are less likely to be included than others. The result? A skewed sample that doesn't truly represent the broader population.

• • •

Stepping into Inclusivity

Inclusivity isn't a destination; it's a journey of continuously ensuring all voices find representation.

1. Diverse Sampling: Ensure that your sample mirrors the diversity of the population. This might mean making extra efforts to reach underrepresented groups.
2. Neutral Questioning: Word your questions neutrally. Avoid leading questions that might push respondents towards a particular answer.
3. Language Sensitivity: If your audience is multi-lingual, consider offering the survey in multiple languages. Remember, language is often the first step to connection.

Tech to the Rescue!

Thankfully, the digital age offers tools and techniques to curb biases. Algorithms can now detect potential biases in questions. Analytics can show if a particular demographic is underrepresented. Use these tools to refine and improve your survey approach.

. . .

Feedback, Feedback, Feedback!

An invaluable strategy to understand if your survey is inclusive is by piloting it within a diverse focus group. Their feedback can help you identify overlooked biases or areas of unintentional exclusion.

Embracing Intersectionality

Inclusivity isn't just about looking at individual identities - be it gender, race, or socio-economic status. It's about understanding the overlaps. A person might belong to multiple marginalized groups, and their experiences can't be understood in isolation. When crafting surveys, embrace this layered perspective.

Reflect, Refine, Repeat

Research is iterative. Every time you conduct a survey, there's room for improvement. Reflect on what worked and what didn't. Where were the gaps? How can you do better next time? Use these reflections to refine your approach.

You know, surveys are like conversations. Just as in a rich, fulfilling chat, you'd want to hear from a variety of perspectives, in survey research, the aim is to capture the kaleidoscope of human experiences. When we reduce biases and promote inclusivity, our findings become richer, deeper, and more meaningful.

Let's pause for a moment. Imagine a world where every research, every survey, every poll genuinely captures the myriad hues of human experience. It's a world where decisions are made based on a holistic understanding, not just the loudest voices. It's a world where everyone feels seen and heard. That's the power of truly inclusive research. And with every survey you craft with care, you're contributing to that vision.

13 / case studies: successes and failures in ux surveys

what we can learn from successful survey campaigns

YOU CLICKED THROUGH, responded with enthusiasm, and by the end, felt a genuine connection to its purpose? It's like having a fantastic coffee chat, where the conversation flows seamlessly, and before you know it, an hour has passed. Now, let's uncover the magic behind those successful survey campaigns and tease out lessons that can transform your next endeavor!

It's All About Engagement

Successful surveys don't just collect data; they engage the respondent. They're like the storytellers of the data world. Here's what they do right:

1. Clear Purpose and Value Proposition: Successful

surveys are crystal clear about their objectives. Respondents know why they're participating and the potential impact of their inputs.

2. Balanced Question Types: A mix of open-ended questions, multiple choice, and scales ensures that the survey remains engaging. Think of it as the varying pitch in a captivating story.

3. Visual Elements: Some of the most memorable surveys integrate visuals, not just to beautify, but to clarify and engage. A well-placed image or infographic can do wonders for understanding.

Respect for the Respondent's Time

Let's face it, no one wants their time wasted, especially not by a never-ending survey. The best ones are succinct, often taking no more than 10-15 minutes. Here's the kicker: they prioritize quality over quantity, diving deep into a few key areas rather than skimming many.

Feedback Loops: A Two-Way Street

The most impactful surveys recognize that data collection is a two-way street. After participants invest their time and insights, they appreciate a summary of findings or even actionable steps taken based on their feedback. It's a sign of respect and acknowledgment.

Optimized for Mobile

In our fast-paced, mobile-first world, ensuring that surveys are mobile-optimized isn't a luxury—it's a necessity. Successful campaigns seamlessly adapt to smaller screens, ensuring a smooth respondent experience.

Transparency and Trustworthiness

Remember our earlier conversation about handling data responsibly? Successful surveys practice what we preached. They're upfront about data usage, ensuring respondents feel safe and secure.

Tailored Invitations and Reminders

Ever received a generic, bland survey request? Now, contrast that with a personalized, well-crafted invitation. Which one are you more likely to click on? Tailored communications can significantly boost response rates.

Real-world Examples: A Quick Dive

Let's look at a couple of instances where surveys knocked it out of the park:

- Airbnb's Host Satisfaction Survey: This regular check-in with hosts isn't just about gathering feedback. Airbnb frames it as a collaboration, where hosts co-create the platform's future. The result? Hosts don't just respond; they engage deeply.

- Spotify's New Feature Feedback: Whenever Spotify tests a new feature, they solicit user feedback. But rather than a generic form, they integrate the survey experience within the app, making it feel like a natural extension of the user journey.

Drawing inspiration from these, can you see how the principles we discussed come alive? It's about blending purpose with engagement, all while respecting the respondent.

Let's imagine you're now prepped to design your next survey. You're weaving in engagement strategies, carefully curating questions, and ensuring transparency. As you pilot the survey, you see excitement in respondents, eagerness to participate. The data flows in, rich and insightful. And as you analyze and act on it, there's a palpable impact.

That's the dream, right? And here's the beautiful part: it's entirely achievable. As you've seen, successful surveys aren't about complex algorithms or flashy designs. They're about connecting, respecting, and engaging. And as someone who's walked this journey, absorbing lessons and insights, you're perfectly poised to create such magic.

pitfalls and lessons from less successful endeavors

We've spent a considerable amount of time pouring over the secrets of those who nailed it. But let's be honest, we learn just as much, if not more, from our missteps. The path to mastery, after all, is often paved with well-intended blunders. This chapter is an homage to those not-so-shiny moments and a deep dive into the lessons they leave behind.

Over-ambition: When More Isn't Merrier

There's something commendable about ambition. But in the survey world, an overzealous approach can backfire. Some surveys try to capture everything, leading to a lengthy and exhausting experience for respondents.

Lesson: Streamline your focus. Decide on the core objectives for your survey and craft questions that align precisely with those goals. Remember, a succinct, impactful survey often trumps an exhaustive one.

Lack of Clarity: The Confounding Conundrum

Ever stumbled upon a survey question that left you scratching your head? Ambiguous, convoluted questions can leave respondents confused, leading to skewed data or, worse, abandoned surveys.

Lesson: Clarity is your best friend. Test your questions with a small group before going live. If they're puzzled, there's a good chance your larger audience might be too.

The Assumption Abyss

Assuming that respondents understand industry jargon or possess background knowledge is a slippery slope. Surveys riddled with assumptions can alienate participants, making them feel out of the loop.

Lesson: Craft questions for everyone. Avoid jargon,

provide context where necessary, and strive to make each respondent feel included in the conversation.

One-size-fits-all Approach

Much like that oversized shirt that you thought would fit just about anyone, a generic survey approach can miss the mark. By not tailoring surveys to specific demographics or user segments, the data collected can often be too broad to yield actionable insights.

Lesson: Segmentation is key. Tailor your surveys to cater to different groups, ensuring that questions resonate and are relevant to each segment.

Ignoring Mobile Users: The Silent Majority

In today's digital age, a staggering number of users access content on their mobile devices. Surveys that aren't optimized for mobile can be a frustrating experience for these respondents, leading to lower participation.

Lesson: Go mobile or go home. Ensure that your surveys are mobile-friendly, providing a seamless experience across devices.

Misleading Data Interpretation

The thrill of seeing data roll in can sometimes lead to hasty conclusions. But cherry-picking data or interpreting it without a comprehensive understanding can lead to misguided actions.

Lesson: Slow down and seek perspectives. Before jumping to conclusions, analyze the data thoroughly, and if possible, get a second pair of eyes on it. Remember, data isn't just numbers; it's a story waiting to be told accurately.

The Feedback Void

Imagine pouring your heart out and then...silence. Many surveys gather invaluable feedback but falter at the crucial step of acknowledging or acting upon it.

Lesson: Close the feedback loop. Communicate the results back to the respondents and let them know how their input is shaping changes. It fosters trust and ensures they're more likely to participate in future surveys.

Real-life Glimpses: When Things Went South

To paint a clearer picture, let's peek at some real-life instances:

- Tech Titan's Feature Feedback Fiasco: A major tech company rolled out a feedback survey for a new feature. However, the survey was riddled with technical jargons, alienating a large chunk of their user base. The feedback was skewed, representing only the tech-savvy segment.

- Retailer's Reward Blunder: A retailer launched a survey promising exclusive discounts. However, due to a glitch, many respondents never received their promised rewards. The oversight not only dented participation rates in subsequent surveys but also impacted brand trust.

Drawing from these examples and the lessons outlined, it becomes clear that while the road to a successful survey is nuanced, the pitfalls are often common and, more importantly, avoidable.

As you reflect on this, remember that every misstep is a stepping stone to greater understanding. In the vast landscape of surveys, it's these lessons, these moments of "Aha! I won't do that again," that refine our approach, sharpen our intuition, and guide us towards crafting surveys that truly resonate.

best practices in action: a look at industry leaders

You know, there's a saying that goes, "Success leaves clues." I've always found this particularly apt when looking at leaders in any field. They set the bar and, in doing so, provide a roadmap for those of us eager to learn, grow, and excel. In the realm of surveys, several industry leaders have left more than just clues—they've left legacy footprints that we can follow. Let's dive deep into their best practices, shall we?

1. Acme Surveys: Keeping it Human

One would think that in a digitized world, surveys would be all about cold numbers and hard facts. But Acme Surveys believes differently. They prioritize human experience. By using conversational language, engaging visuals, and incorporating elements of humor, they've seen a significant uptick in survey completion rates.

What We Can Embrace: A little human touch goes a long way. While keeping it professional, allow warmth and relatability to seep into your surveys.

2. ByteInsight: A Masterclass in Brevity

ByteInsight, a tech analytics firm, is known for its short, impactful surveys. Recognizing the time crunch most professionals face, their surveys often have no more than five questions. But each question is crafted with such precision that they gather more insights than many lengthier surveys.

What We Can Embrace: Quality over quantity. Refine and distill your questions to capture the essence of what you need.

3. GreenScape Feedback Systems: Interactive Elegance

Breaking the monotony of tick boxes and radio buttons, GreenScape introduced interactive elements like sliders, drag and drops, and even AR-based inputs in their surveys. This novel approach transformed the mundane task of survey taking into an almost game-like experience.

What We Can Embrace: Innovation is king. Explore newer, interactive ways to engage respondents, making the process fun for them.

4. RealTalk Inc.: Transparency Triumphs

RealTalk's success lies in their post-survey communications. After gathering feedback, they ensure respondents are informed about the results and subsequent actions. By sharing infographics and summaries, they've cultivated a community of dedicated respondents.

What We Can Embrace: Transparency fosters trust. Share findings and future plans with respondents, making them feel valued and involved.

5. HealthFirst Feedback Systems: Segment Savvy

Recognizing the vast spectrum of their clientele, HealthFirst tailors their surveys to cater to specific demographic segments, like teens, adults, or seniors. This segmented approach yields richer, more relevant insights.

What We Can Embrace: One size doesn't fit all. Customize your surveys for different audience segments to increase relevance.

6. Pangea Insights: The Follow-up Pros

Pangea understands that a survey isn't a one-and-done affair. They have mastered the art of follow-ups, using intelligently timed reminders and incentive structures to ensure maximum participation without being overly intrusive.

What We Can Embrace: Persistence, when done

right, pays off. Strategize your follow-ups to nudge respondents without overwhelming them.

As we traverse these stellar examples, a common thread emerges. Each leader, in their unique way, prioritizes the respondent's experience. They understand that at the heart of every survey is a human being—with emotions, constraints, and preferences.

Imagine being at a gathering. You wouldn't barrage a friend with endless questions, right? Instead, you'd engage in a meaningful conversation, listening as much as you talk. That's the essence these industry leaders capture. They've transformed surveys from a one-way data extraction tool to a two-way dialogue channel.

Emulating these leaders isn't about copying their strategies verbatim. It's about imbibing their ethos. It's recognizing that surveys, in their most elevated form, are platforms for connection, understanding, and growth. When we operate from that space, the best practices naturally flow in, and the impact created resonates far and wide.

14 / continuous improvement and feedback loops

iterating on your survey design

LET'S take a moment to think about our favorite artists—painters, musicians, authors. What sets them apart is not just their masterpieces but their ability to evolve and adapt their craft over time. In many ways, designing a survey is an art form in its own right. And like all art, it's not static. It's dynamic, living, and constantly evolving.

In the previous chapters, we dove deep into the core principles of survey design, learned from industry leaders, and unearthed pitfalls to avoid. But here's a nugget of truth: No matter how meticulously you plan and design your survey, there's always room for enhancement. That's where iteration comes into play.

Why Iteration Matters

Remember the last time you baked something new? Maybe those chocolate chip cookies turned out a tad too crispy, or perhaps the cake could've used a pinch more salt. The beauty is in the baking, trying, tweaking, and trying again until you get it just right.

Similarly, every survey you design is like a fresh batch of cookies. Each response provides insights, not just about the topic in question, but also about the survey itself.

1. Embracing Feedback Loops

Feedback isn't just about the answers to the survey questions. It's also about the questions themselves. Was there a particular question that consistently garnered vague responses? Perhaps another seemed to confuse respondents. These observations are gold mines for refining your questions.

Actionable Tip: Include an optional comment section at the end of your survey. Invite respondents to share feedback about the survey itself. It's amazing what you can learn when you simply ask.

2. Data-Driven Decisions

Iteration isn't about random changes. It's about informed, data-driven refinements. Dive into analytics. Look for patterns. For instance, if a sizable percentage of respondents dropped off at question 7, it's worth revisiting that question to see if it's too complex or perhaps unnecessary.

Actionable Tip: Use visualization tools. A graphical representation of drop-offs, time spent on each question, or other engagement metrics can spotlight areas for improvement.

3. The Power of A/B Testing

One of the most effective ways to iterate is through A/B testing. This involves creating two versions of your survey with slight variations in design, question phrasing, or sequence. By analyzing which version yields better engagement or clearer responses, you can continually refine your approach.

Actionable Tip: Don't change too many variables at once. If you alter the design, question phrasing, and sequence all in one go, pinpointing what led to improved results becomes challenging.

4. Keep Pace with Changing Dynamics

The world isn't static, and neither are its people. Cultural shifts, industry advancements, or even global events can influence perceptions and opinions. Regularly updating your survey to reflect these dynamics ensures that your data remains relevant.

Actionable Tip: Conduct periodic reviews. This doesn't mean overhauling your survey every month. Instead, take stock semi-annually or annually to ensure your questions are still pertinent.

5. Simplicity is Sophistication

Iteration doesn’t always mean addition. Sometimes,

the most impactful change is a subtraction. If certain questions are no longer yielding valuable insights, or if your survey has become too lengthy, trim the fat. A concise, straightforward survey often yields higher engagement.

Actionable Tip: Wear the respondent's shoes. Take your survey yourself or have a colleague do so. A fresh pair of eyes can often spot redundancies or complexities that you might miss.

Let's step back and appreciate the journey. Crafting the perfect survey is not about getting it right the first time. It's about staying committed to the process, embracing feedback, and being willing to pivot when needed. Iteration is the bridge between a good survey and a great one.

And here's a gentle reminder: Every tweak you make is a step forward. It's not just about perfecting a survey, but about the broader goal of understanding, connecting, and making informed decisions.

As we continue this exciting voyage, remember that the art of surveying is ever-evolving. Like a sculptor with clay, you have the power to mold, reshape, and perfect your masterpiece. And with each iteration, you're not just refining a survey—you're honing a skill, refining a craft, and elevating an art form. Happy iterating!

seeking feedback on your survey process

Imagine you've just baked a new type of bread, a recipe you've been tweaking for weeks. You've followed all the right steps, and it looks pretty impressive. But when you offer a slice to someone, they tell you it needs a touch more salt. Now, you could take offense, or you could see this as the missing piece to your perfect loaf.

Likewise, in the world of surveys, the creation process is just half the journey. The other half? It's about constantly seeking feedback, not just on the content of your survey, but on the entire process. Let's delve into why this is vital and how to go about it effectively.

The Why: The Essence of Feedback on Process

Every element of your survey process, from how you frame questions to the manner in which you reach out to respondents, can influence the quality of feedback you receive. By seeking feedback on the process, you ensure that:

1. Respondents feel respected and valued.

2. The survey experience is user-friendly and engaging.

3. The data you gather is genuine, comprehensive, and actionable.

Now, the 'how'. How do you gather this meta-feedback without overwhelming your respondents or clouding the primary data?

1. Embed Checkpoints in the Survey

Consider including a mid-survey checkpoint, perhaps after a section. Pose a simple question like, "How are you finding this survey so far?" Offer a scale or a few options like "Easy to understand", "Too lengthy", or "Questions feel repetitive".

Actionable Tip: Make this feedback optional and assure respondents their input will be used to improve future surveys.

2. Post-Survey Reflections

Once a respondent has submitted their survey, present a short set of questions specifically about their experience. Ask if they found any questions ambiguous, if the flow felt natural, or if there were technical glitches.

Actionable Tip: Keep it brief. You don't want feedback on the process to be a second survey in itself. Three to five pointed questions should suffice.

3. Diversify Your Feedback Channels

While embedding feedback sections within the survey is great, also provide other avenues. An email address where they can send suggestions, a feedback form on your website, or even an open forum can be invaluable.

Actionable Tip: Actively respond to the feedback you receive outside of the survey, even if it's a simple acknowledgment. It fosters trust and encourages more respondents to share their thoughts.

4. Pilot Surveys: The Feedback Goldmine

Before rolling out your survey to the broader audience, conduct a pilot with a smaller group. This isn't just to test the content but also the entire experience. Engage with this group post-survey to gather in-depth feedback. Was the introduction engaging? Were there points where they felt like quitting? Did the visuals aid or distract?

Actionable Tip: Choose a diverse pilot group, ensuring a mix of demographics and tech proficiency. This way, your feedback will be well-rounded.

5. Periodic Review Sessions

Once in a while, bring together a focus group from past respondents. Discuss not just the recent survey but the overarching process. Has it improved? Are there recurring pain points? These sessions can be illuminating, offering insights you hadn't even considered.

Actionable Tip: Make these sessions interactive. Use tools like whiteboards or collaborative digital platforms to map out user journeys and identify friction points.

Let's circle back to our bread analogy. Just as that extra pinch of salt can elevate your loaf from good to exceptional, feedback on your survey process is transformative. It ensures that your survey isn't just a static tool but a dynamic conversation. It acknowledges that while you're seeking answers, you're also open to questions. It's a continuous loop of learning and refining.

staying updated: adapting to changing ux landscapes and user behaviors

Let's set the scene: imagine you've been driving the same route to work every day for the last five years. You know every twist, every turn, and every traffic light's timing by heart. But one day, there's a new road, a fresh diversion, or perhaps an entirely different traffic system in place. If you stubbornly stick to what you knew and resist the change, you might find yourself lost, late for work, or even stuck in a traffic jam.

The world of user experience (UX) isn't all that different. Just as cities evolve and traffic patterns shift, the digital landscape is perpetually morphing, driven by technology's rapid pace and changing user behaviors. If we don't evolve with it, we risk creating experiences that feel outdated or, worse, frustrating for users.

The Winds of Change in UX

The factors causing these shifts in the UX landscape are multifaceted:

1. Technological Advancements: The rise of

augmented reality, voice interfaces, and AI-driven personalization are shaping new interaction paradigms.

2. Cultural Shifts: A greater emphasis on privacy, inclusivity, and accessibility is driving design choices.

3. User Expectations: As users engage with cutting-edge applications, their expectations for speed, convenience, and delight increase across the board.

Now, with this understanding, how do you ensure you're not left behind, clinging to old UX paradigms?

1. Lifelong Learning

Remember when skeuomorphic design (think: those icons that looked like real-life objects) was all the rage? Then flat design took over, and now we're exploring the depths of neumorphism. Stay updated with the latest design trends by:

- Enrolling in courses or attending webinars.
- Participating in UX and design communities.
- Regularly browsing design inspiration sites.

Actionable Tip: Reserve a set time each week for learning. Call it "Future Friday" or "Wednesday Watch" – a dedicated slot to immerse yourself in the new.

2. Usability Testing & Iteration

User behavior is the best predictor of UX success. Regular usability testing can highlight changing preferences or pain points. Maybe users now prefer chatbots for instant answers or love dark mode because it's easier on the eyes.

Actionable Tip: Don't just test new features. Periodically retest old, "established" features to ensure they still meet user expectations.

3. Feedback Loops

Encourage users to provide feedback on their experience. This could be through surveys (which we've extensively discussed!), in-app prompts, or even through user forums. Their insights can often spotlight emerging needs or preferences.

Actionable Tip: Create a feedback-friendly environment. Acknowledge received feedback and, if acted upon, let users know their voice made a difference.

4. Diverse Teams for Diverse Perspectives

A homogenous team might have blind spots. By ensuring your design and development team is diverse in terms of backgrounds, experiences, and skills, you increase the chances of creating a universally appealing UX.

Actionable Tip: Encourage cross-functional workshops. Sometimes, a developer or a marketer might spot a UX trend or need that a designer might miss.

5. Analyzing User Data

Metrics like session duration, bounce rates, and heatmaps can offer clues about user behavior. Perhaps they're not engaging with a new feature, or they're spending a lot of time on a process that should be intuitive. Dive deep into this data to understand and adapt to changing behaviors.

Actionable Tip: Correlate qualitative feedback with quantitative data for a comprehensive view. If users say a page is "confusing," the analytics might show where they drop off, giving you a starting point for improvements.

If you think about it, it's a thrilling challenge. You're not just trying to design for the user of today, but also anticipating the needs and desires of the user of tomorrow. But fear not! With a finger on the pulse of emerging trends and an ear to the ground listening to user feedback, you can navigate these ever-shifting sands.

There's an adage that the only constant in life is change. In the realm of UX, this couldn't be truer. But rather than view it as an obstacle, let's see it as an opportunity: to learn, to adapt, and to create experiences that are not just contemporary but also visionary. After all, while knowing the current traffic patterns is great, envisioning the roads of the future? That's where the real adventure lies.

15 / conclusion: the future of surveys in ux

emerging trends and technologies in survey design

WELL, here we are, diving into the fascinating world of what's new and shiny in survey design. Picture this: You've been using the same trusty hammer and nails for years, and then someone introduces you to a state-of-the-art power drill. The game changes, doesn't it? Likewise, the realm of surveys is bustling with innovation, and today we're setting out to explore this evolving landscape.

1. Conversational Surveys

Gone are the days when surveys felt like tedious school exams. The future is conversational. These surveys mimic a chat interface, asking one question at a time, and often adapting based on the respondent's previous answer. The aim? Making the survey feel like a friendly chat rather than a chore.

Actionable Tip: Tools like Typeform and SurveySparrow can help you design these interactive, conversational surveys.

2. AI-Powered Insights

Enter Artificial Intelligence (AI). With AI, we can now not only analyze survey results faster but also garner deeper insights. This technology can detect patterns, sentiment, and even predict future trends based on respondent data.

Actionable Tip: Don't get overwhelmed with the vastness of AI. Start simple. Use platforms that incorporate AI to analyze open-text answers for sentiment, saving you hours of manual work.

3. Voice and Video Responses

Written responses can sometimes lack the nuance and emotion a voice or video clip can capture. Recognizing this, some platforms now offer respondents the ability to record short voice or video answers. It's like having a face-to-face chat without being in the same room.

Actionable Tip: This approach is particularly handy for detailed feedback where nuances matter. Just remember to ensure respondents know their recordings might be shared or analyzed.

4. VR and AR Surveys

Virtual Reality (VR) and Augmented Reality (AR) aren't just for gamers. These technologies can make surveys more engaging. Imagine asking a respondent to 'walk' through a virtual store and then provide feedback on their experience.

Actionable Tip: While the tech is fantastic, remember that not everyone has access to VR or AR gear. Ensure you have alternative survey methods in place.

5. Mobile-First Design

With the proliferation of smartphones, ensuring your survey looks and feels great on mobile is paramount. It's not just about shrinking your desktop survey; it's about redesigning for thumb-friendly navigation and touch interfaces.

Actionable Tip: Always test your survey on multiple mobile devices before rolling it out. And, consider tools that offer mobile-responsive templates off-the-shelf.

6. Gamified Surveys

Who said surveys can't be fun? Gamification elements, like points, badges, or even simple animations, can boost engagement rates and ensure higher completion rates.

Actionable Tip: While gamifying is fun, ensure it doesn't overshadow the survey's purpose. The goal remains collecting honest, valuable feedback.

7. Integration with Other Tools

Surveys don't live in isolation. They're part of a broader toolkit that professionals like you use every day. Hence, the emergence of platforms that easily integrate with CRM systems, email marketing tools, or even collaboration platforms like Slack.

Actionable Tip: Map out your tech stack. Look for survey tools that can seamlessly integrate, allowing for smoother data flow and analytics.

8. Real-time Reporting and Dashboards

What's the point of collecting feedback if you can't act on it swiftly? Modern survey tools offer real-time dashboards that update as responses roll in, enabling you to spot trends or issues instantly.

Actionable Tip: Ensure your team has access to these dashboards and train them to interpret the data, turning insights into action.

Alright, after that whirlwind tour of the future, you might feel like you've just stepped out of a time machine. The world of survey design is undoubtedly evolving, but remember this: no matter how shiny or advanced the tool, the goal remains the same – understanding and valuing the voice of your respondents.

The crux? While it's exciting to play with new toys, always circle back to the core question: "Will this enhance the respondent's experience and provide me with clearer, actionable insights?" If the answer is yes, dive in. If not, perhaps that shiny new tool is best left on the shelf for now.

the evolving role of surveys in a data-driven world

Imagine, for a moment, a world without questions. A place where nobody asks about your day, how you're feeling, or what you think. Sounds a bit bleak, doesn't it? In essence, that's what a world without surveys would look like—lacking the structured curiosity that helps us understand the nuances of human behavior, needs, and opinions.

But let's zoom out a bit. The digital age is bustling. Every click, swipe, like, or share leaves behind a digital footprint—a plethora of data for businesses to gobble up. Yet, amidst this data avalanche, the humble survey continues to thrive, evolve, and cement its importance. Let's explore why.

The Age of Big Data: Why Surveys Still Matter

In a universe brimming with automated analytics and big data, one might wonder, "Do we still need to ask questions when so much is automatically tracked and logged?"

Well, data might tell you what is happening, but surveys help illuminate the why. For instance, analytics can indicate a sudden drop in a product's sales, but a well-crafted survey might reveal it's due to a new competitor or perhaps a misplaced marketing message.

Contextualizing Raw Data

Think of big data as the broad strokes on a canvas, while survey data adds the intricate details and shading. Analytics might tell you that users spend a mere 30 seconds on a new feature of your app, but a survey could tell you they found it confusing or redundant.

Quick Tip: Whenever you spot an anomaly or trend in your analytics, consider deploying a targeted survey to dig deeper into the causative factors.

Humanizing Data Points

Numbers can sometimes dehumanize experiences. Behind every data point is a human with emotions, opinions, and motivations. Surveys bring back the human voice into the equation. They turn impersonal statistics into relatable stories, which can be pivotal in shaping business strategies that resonate on a human level.

Predicting Future Trends

While historical data can provide patterns, survey data, especially when gathered regularly, can be a window into future behaviors and preferences. By continually asking about users' needs, desires, and pain points, businesses can stay one step ahead, anticipating market shifts and evolving preferences.

Surveys in the Age of Social Media

Social media has amplified the voice of the consumer. A single tweet or review can influence public opinion. In this environment, surveys can serve as a proactive tool, allowing businesses to gauge sentiment before it becomes a trending hashtag.

Quick Tip: Consider embedding short, snappy surveys within social media channels to engage users where they already are.

Personalization and the Rise of Tailored Surveys

The modern consumer expects personalization. They're more likely to engage with content (or surveys) tailored to their interests and past behaviors. With advancements in AI and machine learning, dynamic surveys that adapt to the respondent's answers are becoming the norm, not the exception.

Feedback Loops and Continuous Improvement

The agile mindset isn't just for software development. In a rapidly changing market landscape, the businesses that thrive are those that iterate and adapt. Surveys are pivotal in this continuous feedback loop, ensuring that change is always rooted in user needs and feedback.

Alright, let's pause for a breath. By now, you might be thinking, "Alright, surveys are essential, but how do we ensure they stay relevant in this fast-paced, data-heavy world?"

Great question! It's not about discarding old methods, but about integrating the traditional with the new. Use the rich insights from big data to inform your survey design. Understand the broader trends, and then use surveys to fill in the gaps, to add depth and context.

And remember, as much as our world becomes increasingly digitized, the human element remains paramount. People want to be heard. They want to share their stories, experiences, and suggestions. Surveys provide them with this platform.

In a nutshell, as we navigate this data-driven world, the role of surveys is not diminishing; it's simply evolving. It's shifting from a standalone feedback tool to an integrated, strategic instrument that, when combined with other data sources, offers a 360-degree view of the consumer.

preparing for the next wave of ux research methodologies

As waves relentlessly crash upon the shore, so too does the ever-evolving tide of User Experience (UX) research methodologies. Just when you think you've mastered the current methodologies, the digital horizon hints at something new, challenging, and exciting. The world of UX is dynamic, and its research methods are no different. Let's dive deep and ride the wave together, understanding how we can best prepare for what's coming next.

A Quick Trip Down Memory Lane

Not too long ago, UX research was mostly about usability testing. Participants were observed while they interacted with a product, and researchers jotted down where they stumbled. Fast forward a few years, and now we're integrating biometric sensors, virtual reality, and even AI-driven analytics into our research methods.

Why The Constant Evolution?

Simple—technology is always changing, and so are user behaviors. Our devices have transformed, and with them, our expectations and the way we interact with digital interfaces. These shifts necessitate new methods of understanding and improving the user experience.

The Digital Frontier: What's On The Horizon?

1. Emotional Analytics: Beyond traditional usability testing, emotional analytics use facial recognition, voice analysis, and biometric sensors to gauge a user's emotional response to a product. By understanding emotions like frustration, joy, or confusion, we can design more intuitive and engaging experiences.

2. Immersive Experiences with AR & VR: Augmented Reality (AR) and Virtual Reality (VR) are no longer just buzzwords—they're becoming integral

to UX research. With these tools, we can put users in realistic, simulated environments, allowing for richer feedback and insights.

3. Predictive User Experience: With the growth of machine learning and AI, we're moving towards a realm where we can predict user behavior based on historical data. This means UX research won't just be about understanding the present but also forecasting the future.

Getting Ready for The Wave: How Do You Prepare?

Stay Curious: This might sound cliché, but the foundation of any UX researcher should be an insatiable curiosity. Read widely, attend conferences, join webinars, and keep an ear to the ground.

Invest in Training: As methodologies evolve, training becomes crucial. Whether it's a course on emotional analytics or a workshop on VR in UX research, continuous learning is the key.

Collaborate: UX research is becoming increasingly interdisciplinary. Collaborate with data scientists, neurologists, or even psychologists. Their expertise can offer fresh perspectives and deepen the research.

Ethical Considerations: With advanced methodologies, ethical considerations become even more critical. For example, when using biometric sensors or facial recognition, ensure user consent and data privacy.

Adopt a Hybrid Approach: While it's essential to

embrace the new, don't discard the old. Traditional methods like surveys or interviews still have their place. The magic often lies in combining the old with the new for a holistic understanding.

Embrace Failure: Not every new methodology or tool will be a perfect fit. Sometimes, you might need to try out a few before finding the one that aligns with your research needs. Embrace these learning opportunities.

Alright, let's take a moment here. Feels overwhelming? It can be. But think of it as a thrilling journey. Each new methodology is like a new destination, offering fresh landscapes and insights.

The Bigger Picture

Amidst this flurry of emerging methodologies, let's not lose sight of the essence of UX research—it's about understanding the user. Whether you're using the most advanced biometric sensors or a simple paper survey, the end goal remains the same: crafting experiences that resonate, engage, and delight.

It's also worth noting that as we stand at the cusp of these advancements, there's an inherent responsibility. The power these tools wield is immense. Using them ethically, responsibly, and judiciously is as crucial as the insights they provide.

Change can be daunting, but it's also invigorating. It offers new challenges, fresh perspectives, and a chance to reinvent. So, as we stand on the shoreline, watching the next wave of UX research methodologies approach, let's not just brace ourselves. Instead, let's dive in headfirst, ready to explore the depths and harness the momentum to propel us forward. After all, the world of UX waits for no one, and there's no time like the present to gear up and ride the wave. Ready to make a splash?

appendices

survey tool recommendations

If you've ever tried to fix a car with a butter knife or open a wine bottle with a shoe (trust me, some people have tried), you'll know that having the right tools for the task is not just handy—it's essential. Similarly, in the vast universe of user research, having the best survey tool at your disposal can make all the difference. Now, while I can't help with car repairs or wine bottle hacks, I've got you covered on the survey front!

Why the Right Tool Matters

Remember our chat about UX trends and adapting to evolving methodologies? As the world of user experience grows, so does the need for specialized tools to capture nuanced data. But with an ocean of options out there, how do you fish out the perfect tool for your needs? Fret not, let's navigate these waters together.

Dive Into the Toolbox

1. Typeform: If you're looking for something visually appealing and conversational, Typeform is your go-to. With its interactive interface, it not only captures data but also keeps respondents engaged. It's particularly useful when targeting a younger, tech-savvy audience.

2. SurveyMonkey: A classic choice for many. SurveyMonkey offers a plethora of question types and is known for its robust analytics. Whether you're a beginner or a seasoned pro, its user-friendly interface won't let you down.

3. Qualtrics: For those who love diving deep into data, Qualtrics offers advanced analysis options, including cross-tabulation and text analysis. It's especially suited for complex research projects where data granularity matters.

4. Google Forms: On a tight budget? Google Forms might be your savior. While it might lack some of the bells and whistles of premium tools, it's straightforward, free, and integrates seamlessly with other Google products.

5. SurveyGizmo (now Alchemer): A versatile tool that scales with your needs. From simple polls to intri-

cate multi-page surveys, SurveyGizmo offers flexibility without compromising on depth.

6. Microsoft Forms: For those nestled in the Microsoft ecosystem, Microsoft Forms offers integration with Office 365. It's simple, clean, and does the job, especially for quick internal surveys.

Choosing the Right Tool for YOU

With this toolbox at hand, how do you pick the one? Here are a few considerations:

- Budget: Some tools offer robust features at a premium, while others are free or come with a nominal charge.

- Complexity: Are you running a quick poll or an extensive study? Tools like Qualtrics shine for intricate surveys, but for simpler ones, Google Forms might suffice.

- Audience: Think about who will be filling out your survey. For a tech-savvy crowd, interactive platforms like Typeform might be engaging. But for a diverse audience, the simplicity of SurveyMonkey might be better.

- Integration: If you're already using a set of tools (like Google Workspace or Office 365), you might want a survey tool that fits snugly within your existing workflow.

Remember, the best tool is the one that aligns with your specific needs. It's worth taking a few for a spin, experimenting, and figuring out which one feels just right.

Some Pro Tips as You Venture Forth

a. Always Pilot: Before launching your survey, test your chosen tool with a smaller audience. It helps in understanding any hiccups in the tool or the survey itself.

b. Stay Updated: Tools evolve. Features get added, interfaces change, pricing models get revised. Ensure you're always on top of these changes.

c. Community and Support: Often overlooked, but having a vibrant community or robust customer support can be a lifesaver, especially when you hit a roadblock.

sample survey questions for various ux scenarios

Just like a chef needs the right ingredients to whip up a gourmet meal, a researcher requires thoughtfully framed questions to gather meaningful data. Dive in with me as we explore an array of sample questions tailored to different UX scenarios. And, just like a secret family recipe, these questions can serve as your starting point, ready to be tweaked and customized as per your unique needs.

1. Website Usability

When gauging the usability of your website, the key is to understand if users can accomplish what they set out to do and how effortlessly they can do it.

- How easy was it for you to navigate our website?
- On a scale of 1-10, how would you rate the clarity of the information presented?
- Were there any areas / pages where you felt lost or confused?
- Did the website load quickly enough for you?
- Were you able to complete your task or find the information you were seeking?

2. Mobile App Experience

Mobile apps have their unique challenges, from limited screen real estate to ensuring smooth inter-activity.

- How satisfied are you with the speed of our app?
- Are there any features in the app that you found unnecessary or redundant?
- On a scale of 1-5, how intuitive were the app's controls and gestures?
- How would you describe the overall visual appeal of the app?
- Were there moments when the app crashed or hung unexpectedly?

3. E-commerce Shopping Experience

E-commerce sites need to ensure a seamless journey from browsing products to the final checkout.

- How easy was it to search for products?
- Did product descriptions and images match your expectations?
- How would you rate the checkout process?
- Were payment gateways secure and efficient?
- Would you recommend our e-commerce site to a friend?

4. Feedback on New Features

If you've rolled out a new feature or tool, understanding its reception is paramount.

- How often do you use [new feature]?
- What challenges, if any, did you face while using [new feature]?
- How has [new feature] added value to your overall experience?
- Are there aspects of [new feature] that felt unnecessary?
- Any suggestions for improving [new feature]?

5. Content Evaluation

For platforms focused on delivering content, whether it's a blog, news site, or e-learning platform.

- How relevant did you find our content to your needs or interests?
- Were there topics you wish we covered more extensively?
- How would you describe the readability and presentation of our content?

- Did any piece of content stand out as particularly engaging or unappealing?

- How do you generally consume our content? (e.g., reading on mobile, watching videos, etc.)

Now, while these questions serve as a great starting point, here are a few universal tips to make them even more effective:

- Be Clear and Concise: Ambiguity is the nemesis of a good survey. Make sure your questions are clear and to the point.

- Avoid Leading Questions: Keep personal bias at bay. For instance, instead of asking "Don't you think our app is user-friendly?", ask "How would you rate the user-friendliness of our app?"

- Offer Scaled Responses: Providing a scale (like 1-5 or 1-10) often captures nuance better than a simple yes/no.

- Open-Ended vs. Closed: While closed questions (those with fixed answers) are easier to analyze, open-ended ones can offer deeper insights. Balance is the key.

Imagine your survey as a casual chat with your users over a cup of coffee. Your aim? To listen, understand, and evolve. Each question is an opportunity to delve deeper into their minds, to see your product or service through their eyes. And remember, while these sample questions are a sturdy scaffold, don't hesitate to mold them, twist them, and make them truly yours.

As you venture into your next UX research expedition with these questions in tow, picture the insights they'll unravel, the stories they'll tell, and the paths they'll illuminate. All the best, and here's to many more insightful conversations with your audience!

resources for further learning

If the journey we've embarked on together throughout this book has sparked your passion for delving even deeper into the world of user experience and survey design, I have some good news: the learning doesn't have to stop here! Picture this chapter as a treasure map, pointing you towards the gold mines of information where you can further hone your skills. From insightful books to online courses and communities, let's navigate this ever-evolving landscape of knowledge together.

Books That Illuminate the Path

Ah, the timeless charm of books! Here are a few curated recommendations that promise to be a delightful and enriching read:

1. "Don't Make Me Think" by Steve Krug: A classic in UX design, this book unravels the principles of intu-

itive navigation and web usability. Krug's witty style will not only inform you but entertain you as well.

2. "The Design of Everyday Things" by Don Norman: Ever wondered why some products delight users while others frustrate them? Norman dives deep into the psychology of design in this seminal work.

3. "Measuring the User Experience" by William Albert and Thomas Tullis: A deep dive into quantifying the user experience, this book is perfect for those who love numbers and analytics.

Online Courses to Sharpen the Saw

The internet is brimming with platforms offering courses tailored to every learning style:

1. Coursera's "Interaction Design Specialization" by University of California: This comprehensive course will walk you through the nuances of human-computer interaction.

2. Udemy's "User Experience (UX): The Ultimate Guide to Usability and UX": A practical, project-based course that's perfect for hands-on learners.

3. LinkedIn Learning's "UX Foundations: Usability Testing": Dive into the intricacies of usability testing and learn from real-world examples.

Podcasts for the Curious Mind

Who said learning can't be done on the go? Pop in those earbuds and tune into some insightful conversations:

1. "The UX Podcast": Hosted by James Royal-Lawson and Per Axbom, this podcast blends interviews with discussions on a variety of UX topics.

2. "User Defenders": This one dives into the personal journeys of UX professionals, offering both inspiration and insights.

Communities and Forums: The Heartbeat of Collaboration

Joining a community can be a game-changer. It allows you to share insights, ask questions, and stay updated on the latest trends:

1. UX Design.cc: Beyond its treasure trove of articles, it boasts an active community where you can engage in discussions or seek feedback.

2. Reddit's r/userexperience: A bustling forum where novices and experts come together to discuss challenges, share resources, and more.

3. Meetup.com: Look for local UX and interaction design groups. Nothing beats face-to-face networking and learning!

Conferences and Workshops

Immersion in a workshop or conference environment can do wonders:

1. Nielsen Norman Group's Usability Week: Renowned for their in-depth workshops and networking opportunities.

2. UX Week: A mix of inspiring talks and hands-on workshops that promise a holistic learning experience.

3. Local UX Workshops: Keep an eye out for workshops happening in your city or region. Local chambers of commerce or design schools often host them.

Mentorship: The Guiding Star

Never underestimate the value of having a mentor. Platforms like MentorNet or ADPList can connect you with experienced UX professionals eager to guide budding enthusiasts.

www.ingramcontent.com/pod-product-compliance
Lightning Source LLC
LaVergne TN
LVHW090356210926
848480LV00002B/362

* 9 7 9 8 2 2 3 5 3 2 6 1 3 *